BIG HEAD MONSTERS

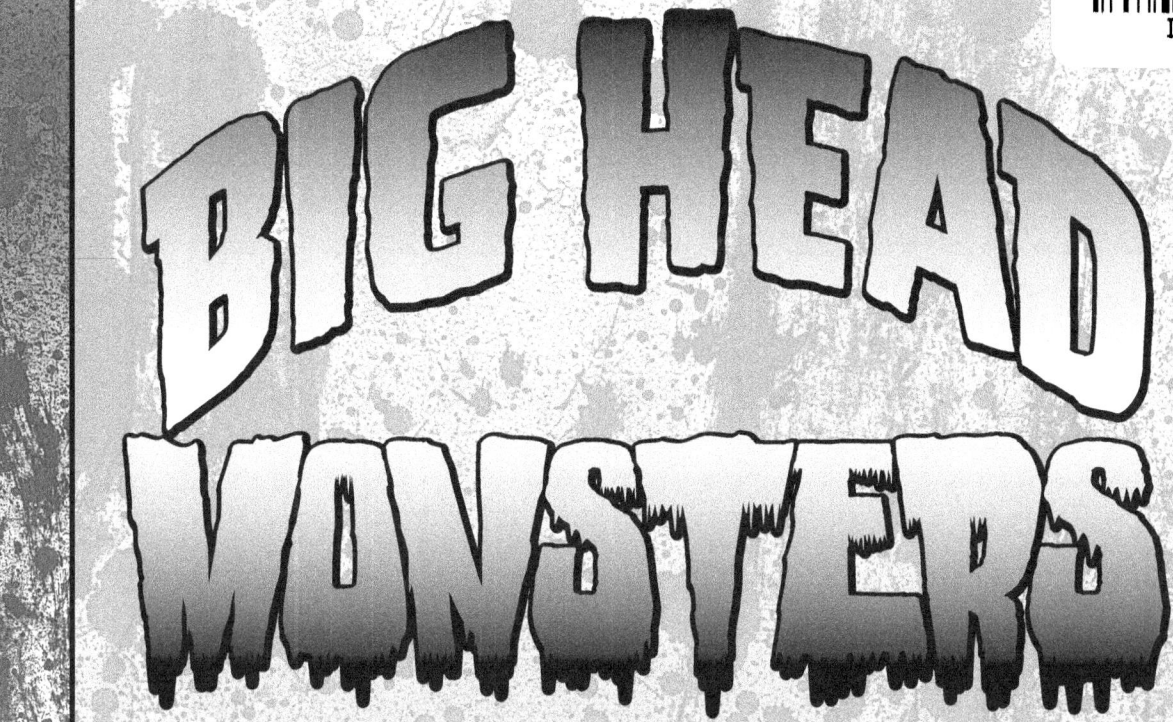

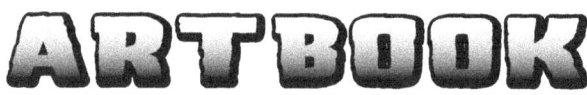
ARTBOOK

Local Sacramento artist Neil Riehle has been working as a professional illustrator and designer for 30 years. Developing his cartooning skills as a T-shirt artist in the early '80s, he continues to sketch illustrations for business and pleasure. He has worked as a graphic designer creating advertising and marketing materials, and was a partner in his own graphic design business for several years. He has produced work as a commercial artist for projects that include brochure & book design, magazine & periodical advertising, web design, 3D & multimedia graphics, animation, and cartoons & comic strips.

From an early age he has had an interest in comic books. He began to collect them as a teenager, fascinated in the art of storytelling with drawings. Planning to make a profession as a comic book artist, he attended art school. After leaving school, he found his way to Sacramento and began his art career there. Today, with several projects in the works, he is developing new characters & stories and continues to hone his comic book art skills. Much of his work can be found on various sites on the internet.

Self-published comic books of his work include: RANDOM EYE SPOTLIGHT, WALLOP! and THE REMAINZ. You can see more illustrations on splashpages.com, Facebook, DevaintArt and Pinterest.

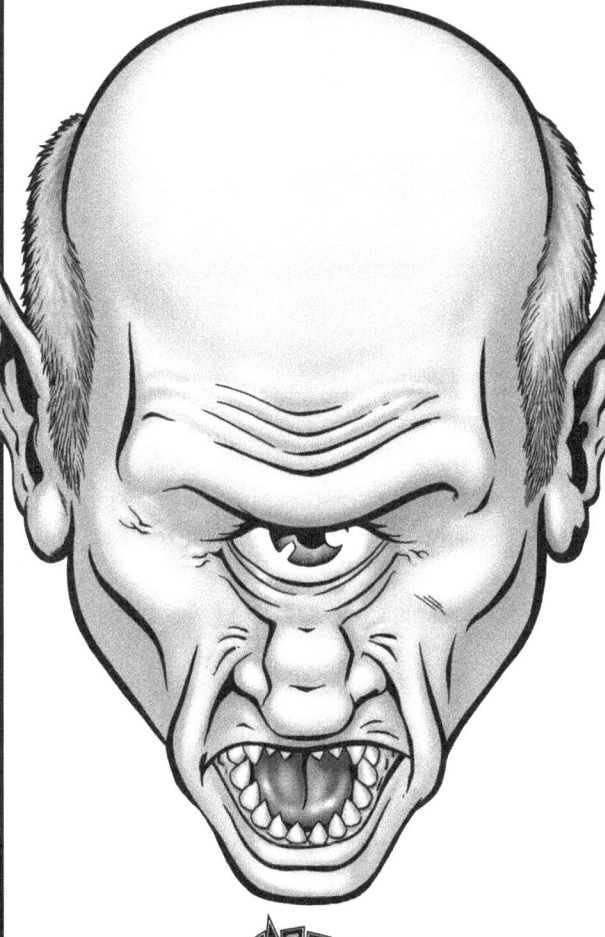

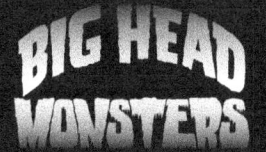

Drawings & Rhymes by
NEIL RIEHLE

Edited by
SR STEWART

Printed by CreateSpace

INTRODUCTION

The plan to draw a monster a week started out simply enough. I began to draw home-made post cards to send to friends and family, and cartoons of monsters seemed to be the most interesting subject to produce. The first cards I made had images of the Mummy, Frankenstein's creature, Dracula, etc, and in keeping with caricature protocol, I made them all with large, exaggerated heads.

I never ended up mailing them. However, I was pleased with the drawings and enjoyed doing them. After that, I began to draw more refined images of monsters in my sketchbooks. I inked finished versions on larger sized, higher quality paper, and colored them with water color paints. I gave the finished color artwork to some of my siblings. It was fun and felt fulfilling.

It wasn't long after that beginning that I came up with an idea to make a series of monster drawings and collect them in a book, complete with written descriptions of each creature and facts and fables related to them. I started sketching various monsters in my sketchbook, and when I was satisfied with the drawing, I'd ink them on bristol board. I started working on the layout of the book, and wrote some of the text I would need after researching the subject on the internet. However, other priorities began to demand my attention, and the book didn't get very far.

Then, as the year of 2013 drew to a close, I decided I wanted to challenge myself to see if I could create a finished drawing each week to post on the internet. I've considered producing an online comic, and I thought I should test myself before committing to such an endeavor. Posting a drawing of a monster each week seemed doable, and, after the first of the year of 2014, I began to do just that. I was fortunate to have a series of backups if I was unable to make the weekly deadline, and held most of those in reserve until the final weeks.

One of the hardest parts of the project was coming up with subjects to draw. I began making lists of all of the creatures, myths and legends I could think of, and scheduled them to be posted on predetermined dates. I decided some of them would work nicely with specific holidays, such as a witch on Halloween, or Marley's ghost at Christmas, but, for the most part, each posting was random.

I began including a rhyme with each drawing after about a month. It started out quite by accident, as one of the captions I wrote had a peculiar rhyme to it. For this book, I've gone back and written rhymes for those monsters that originally didn't have one, added lines to some, and modified or rewrote others. It's not Shakespeare, but I felt the rhymes added a little extra to the plain image of characters.

Now that the project is done, I have time to work on other projects that have been languishing on my desktop for far too long. All of these drawings can still be seen on Facebook by searching for Wallop Comics. I have also posted the images on DeviantArt and Pinterest. I welcome all to visit these sites to view my cartoons and see what new things I have been working on.

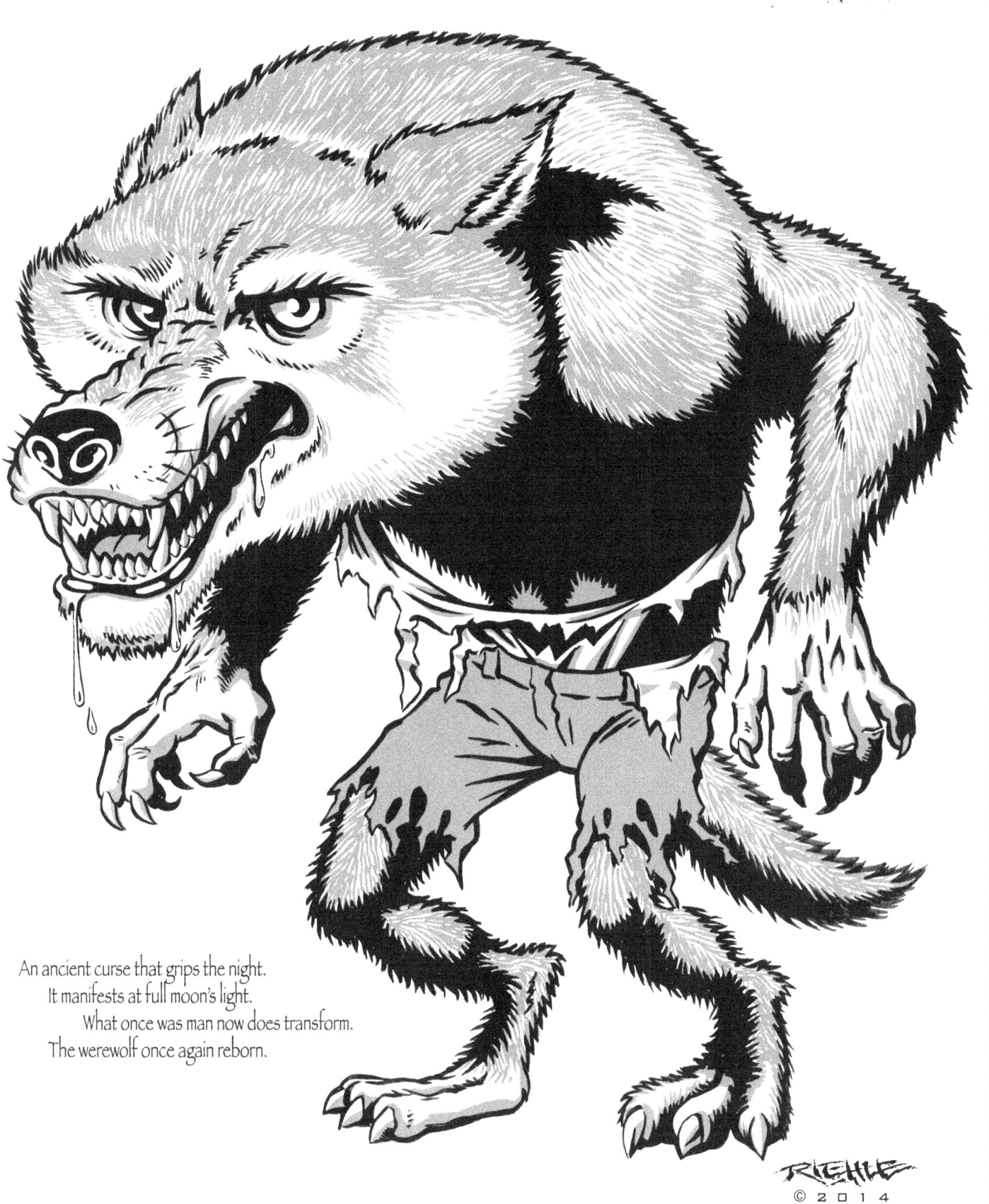

An ancient curse that grips the night.
It manifests at full moon's light.
What once was man now does transform.
The werewolf once again reborn.

RIEHLE
© 2 0 1 4

Bigfoot

It disappears without a trace,
catch not a glimpse from quickened pace.
Though rarely seen, few have observed
those footprints left in soil preserved.

RIEHLE
© 2 0 1 4

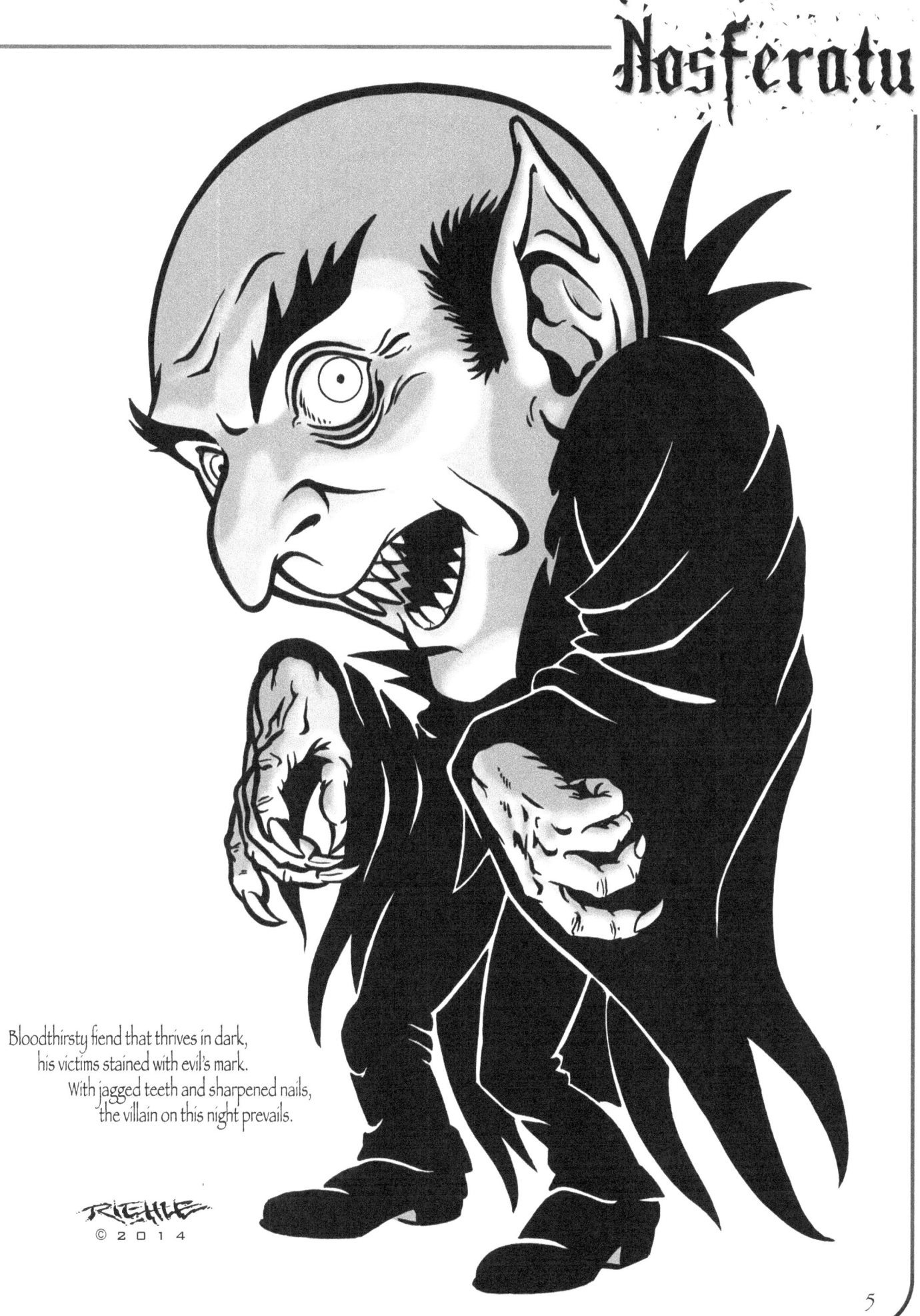

Bloodthirsty fiend that thrives in dark,
his victims stained with evil's mark.
With jagged teeth and sharpened nails,
the villain on this night prevails.

RIEHLE
© 2014

Cthulhu

Dimensions alien can hold,
elder gods, extremely old.
Lovecraft knew the psyche brings
release of vile, hideous things.

RICHLE
© 2 0 1 4

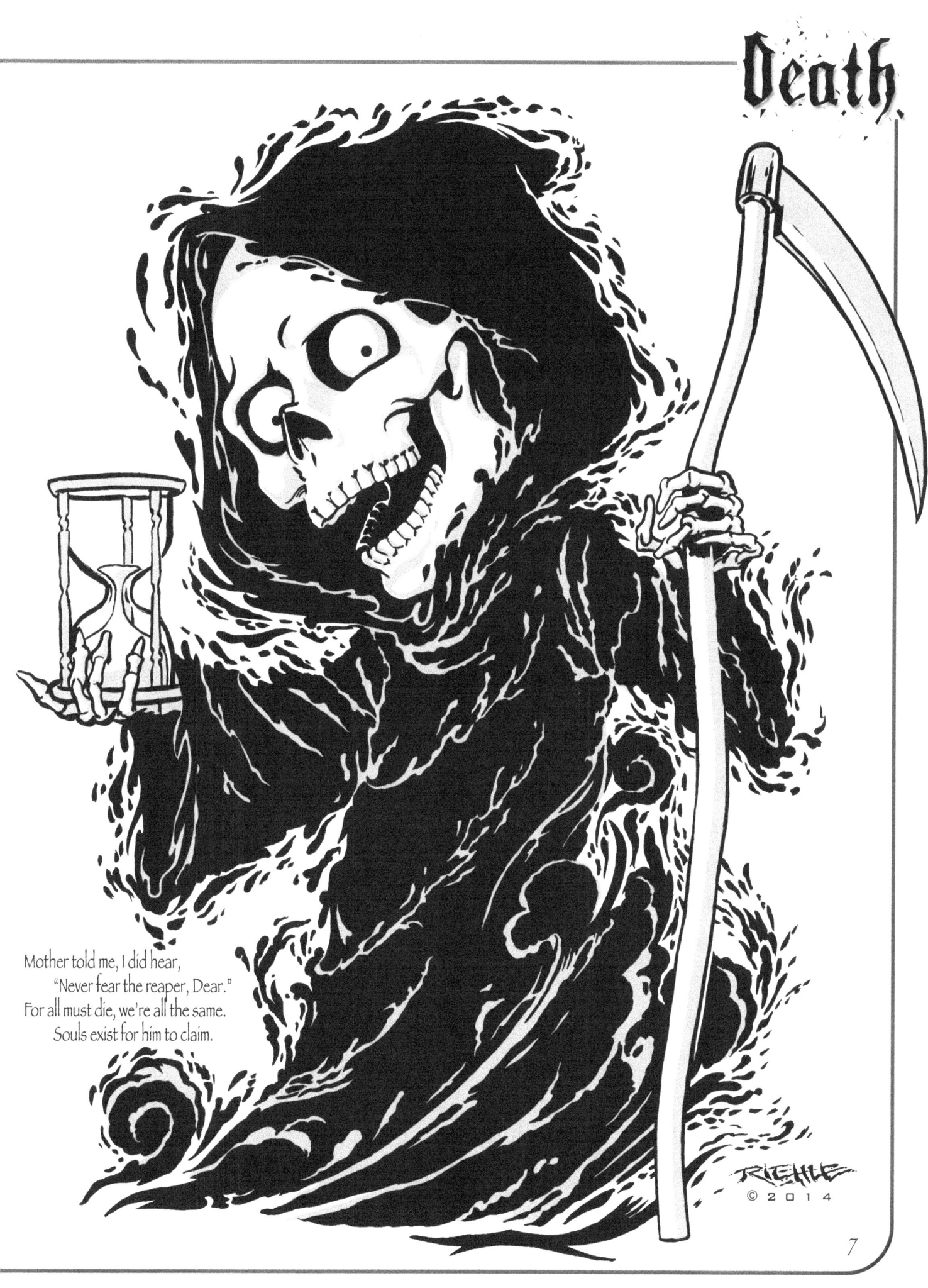

Mother told me, I did hear,
"Never fear the reaper, Dear."
For all must die, we're all the same.
Souls exist for him to claim.

Jekyll & Hyde

A potion brewed in science name,
to split the soul, one brute, one tame.
The balanced mind is overcame
when savage lust is lit aflame.

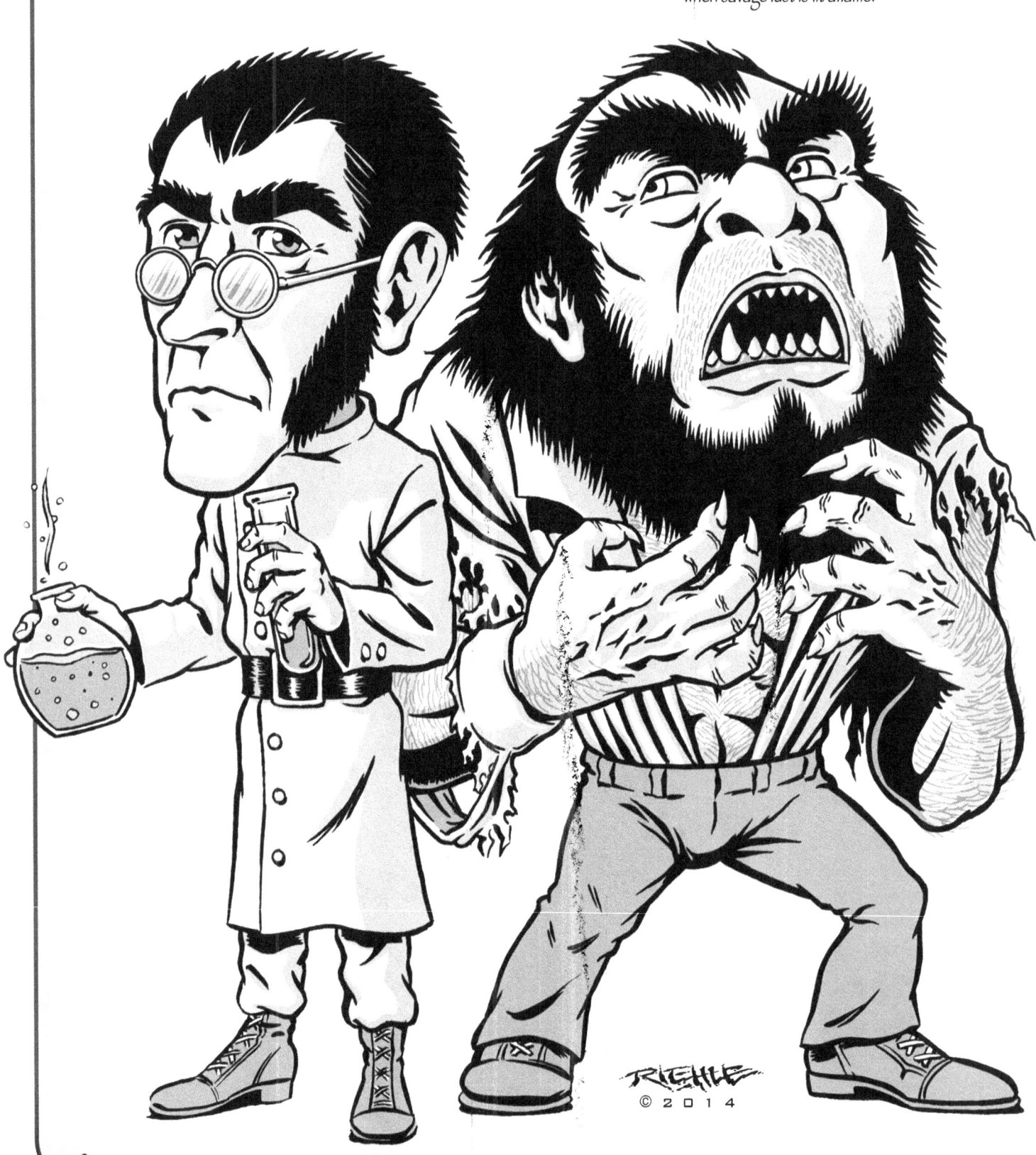

Toxic spills, radioactive landfills,
here's the product of our modern day's ills.
Take note, take heed, this path's not wise
we gamble with our own demise.

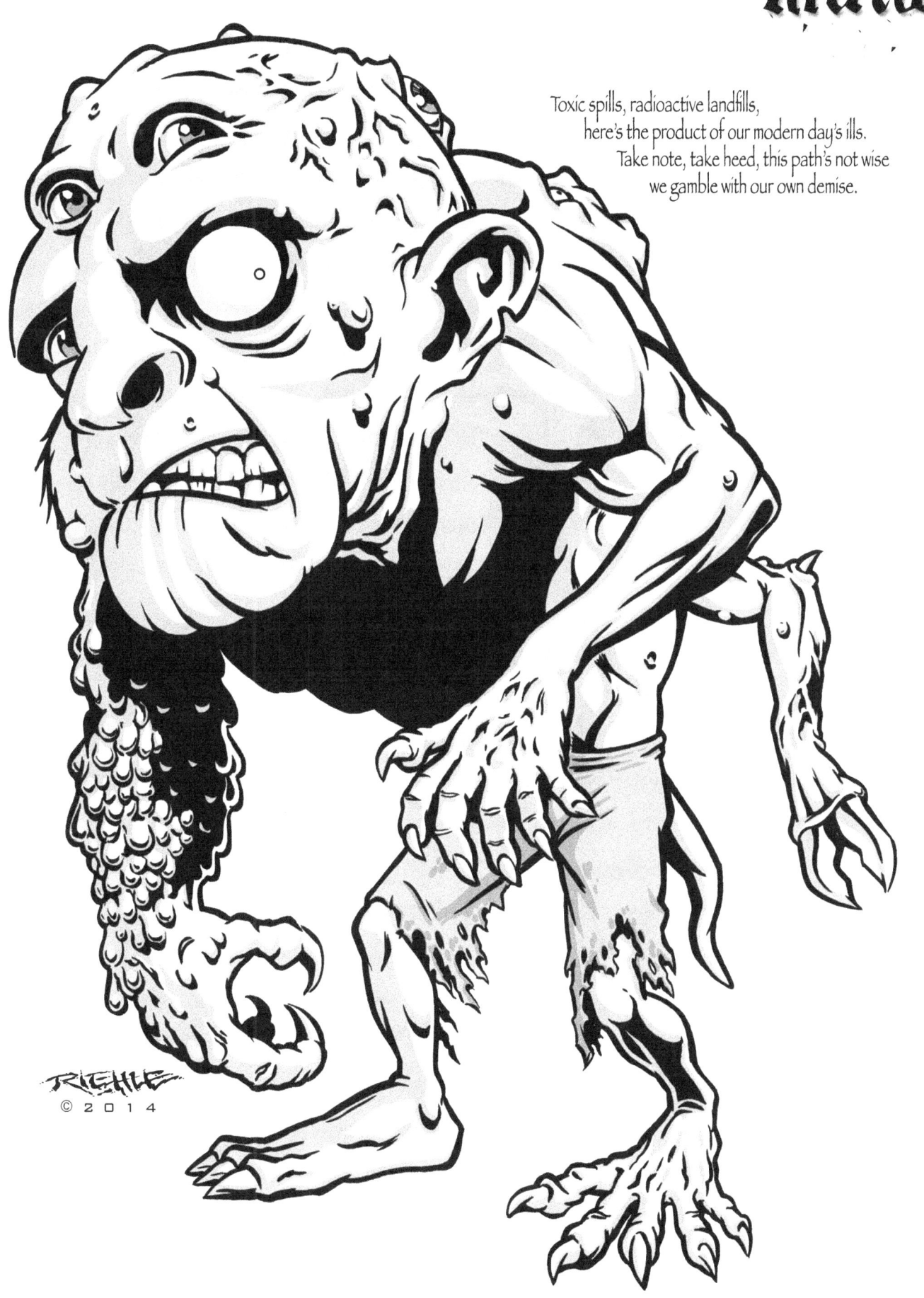

RIEHLE
© 2 0 1 4

Goblin

A Goblin's heart, so full of greed,
covets what he doesn't need.
Gold and jewels he longs for most
and grip his mind, deeply engrossed.

RIEHLE
© 2 0 1 4

Bug Eyed Monster

By accident, this science explorer
is transformed to a walking horror!
No process known can change his fate
forever more this gruesome state.

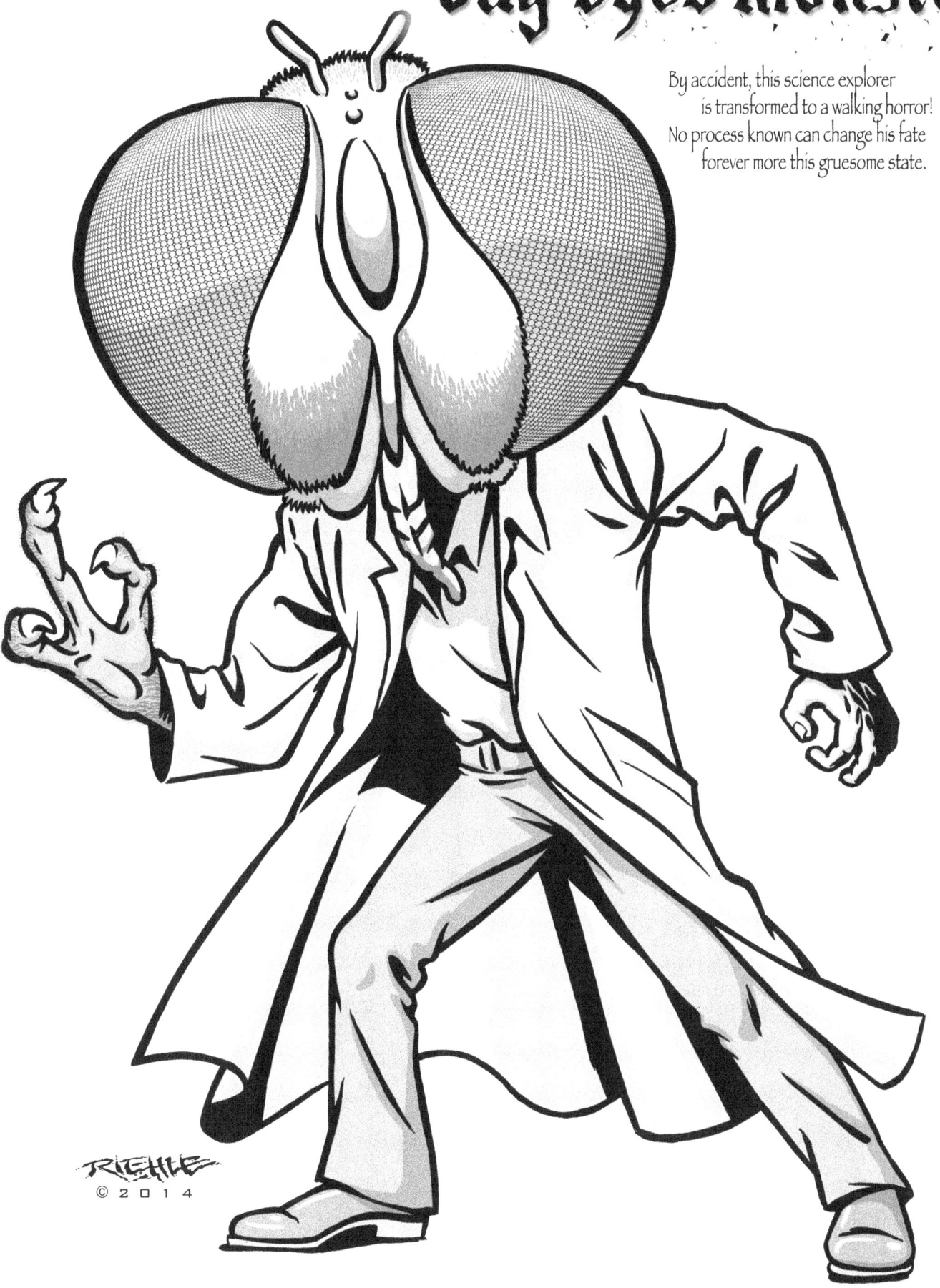

RIEHLE
© 2 0 1 4

Sorceress

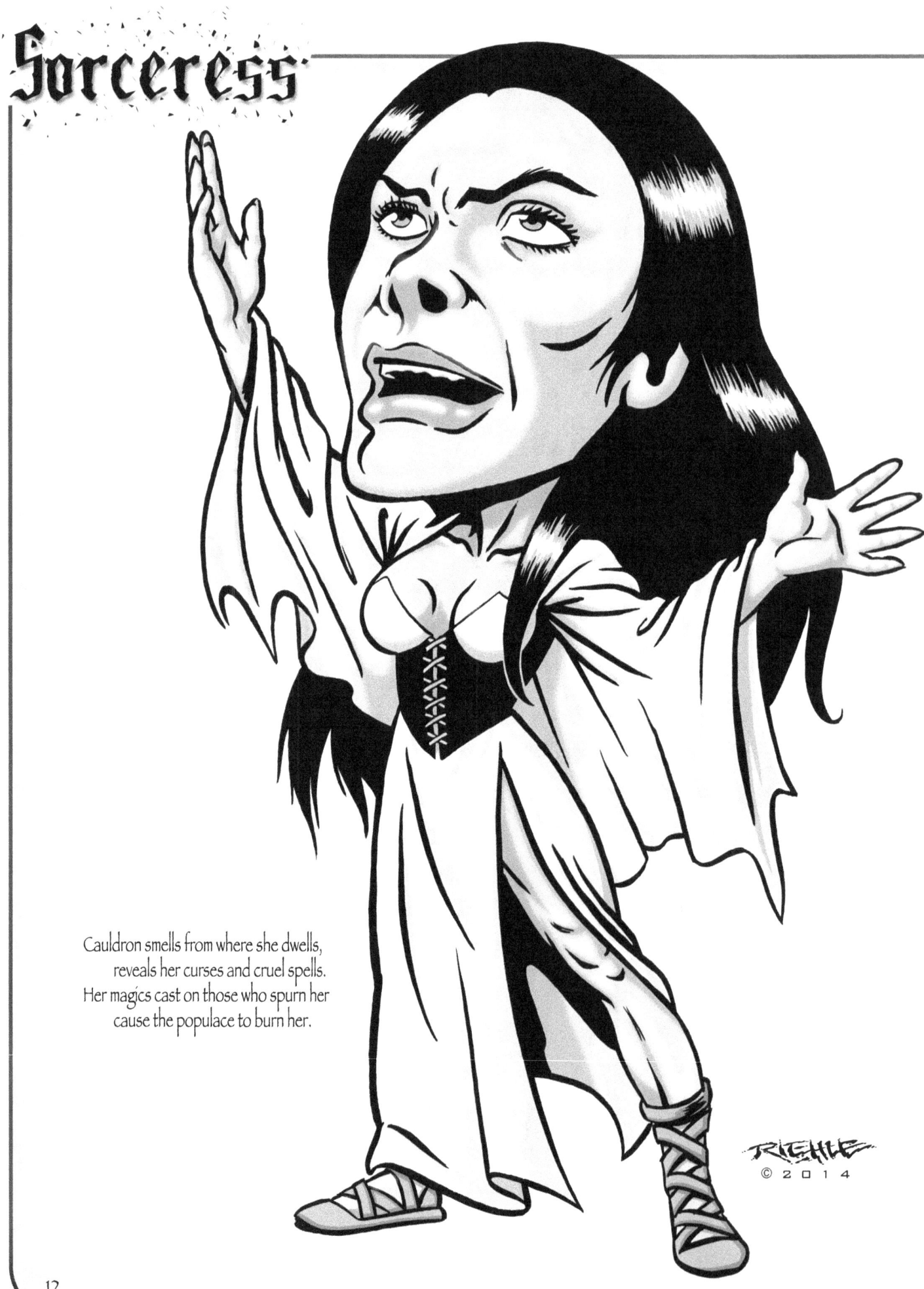

Cauldron smells from where she dwells,
reveals her curses and cruel spells.
Her magics cast on those who spurn her
cause the populace to burn her.

RICHILE
© 2 0 1 4

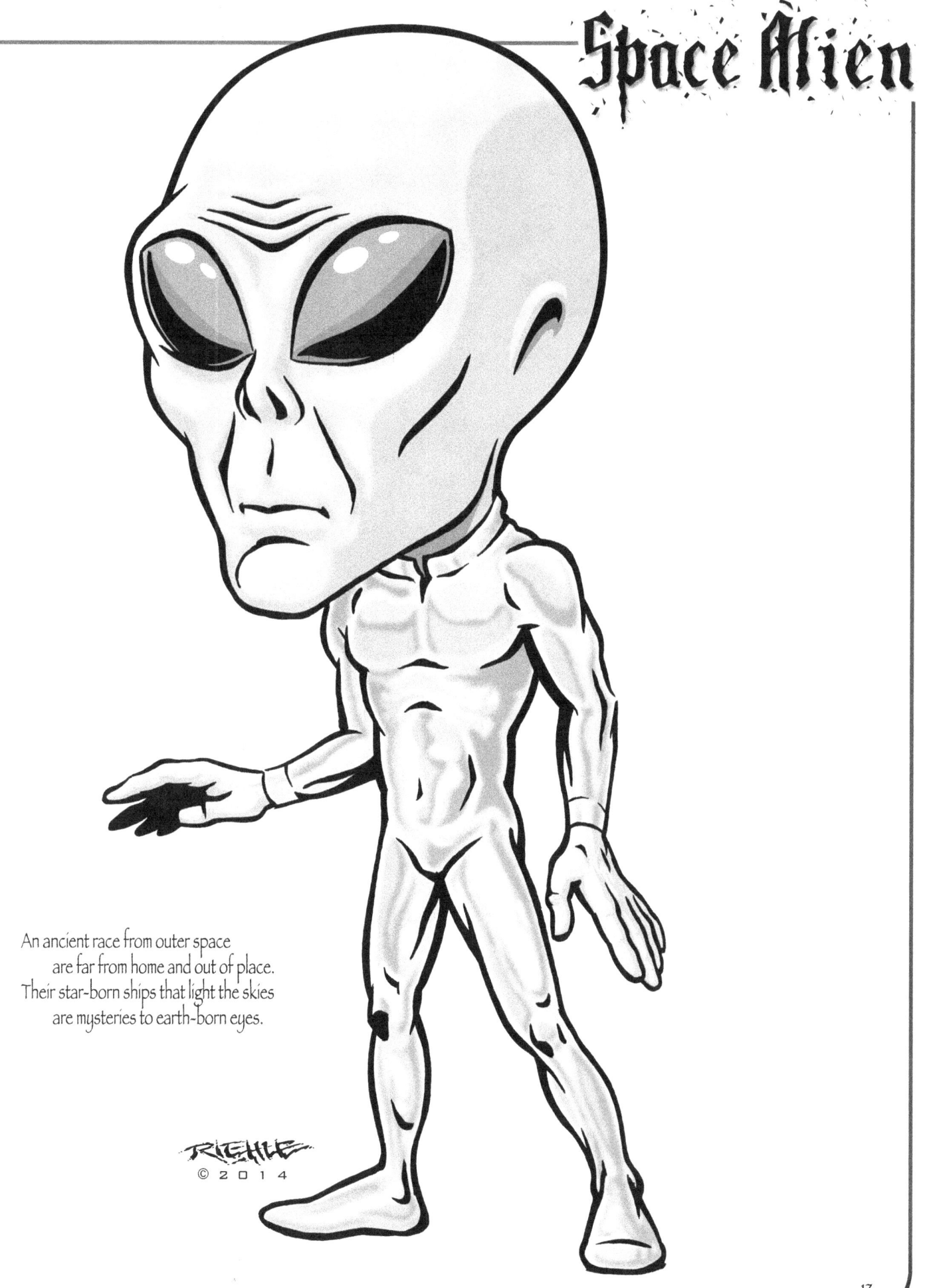

An ancient race from outer space
are far from home and out of place.
Their star-born ships that light the skies
are mysteries to earth-born eyes.

RIEHLE
© 2 0 1 4

Ogre

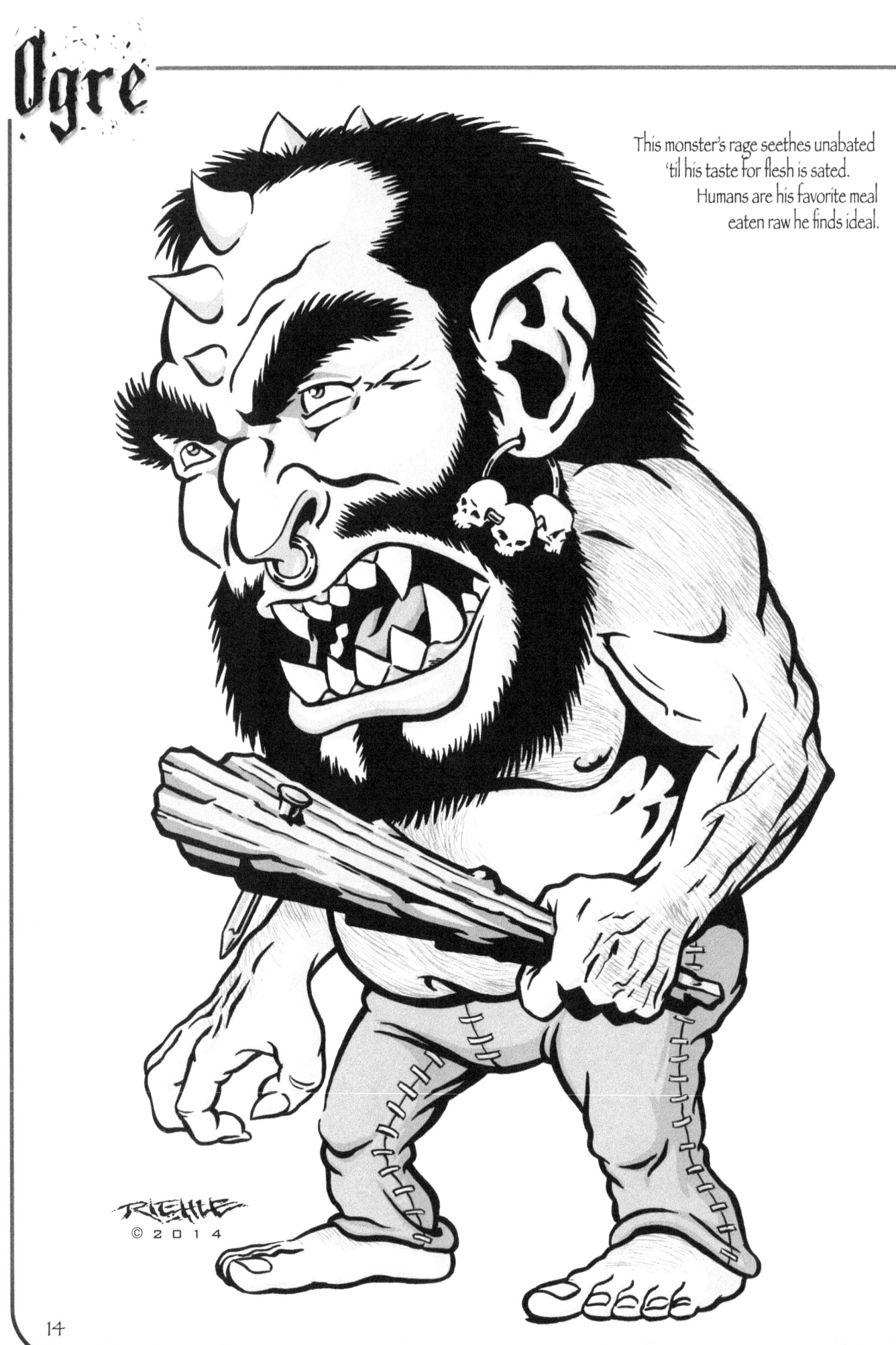

This monster's rage seethes unabated
'til his taste for flesh is sated.
Humans are his favorite meal
eaten raw he finds ideal.

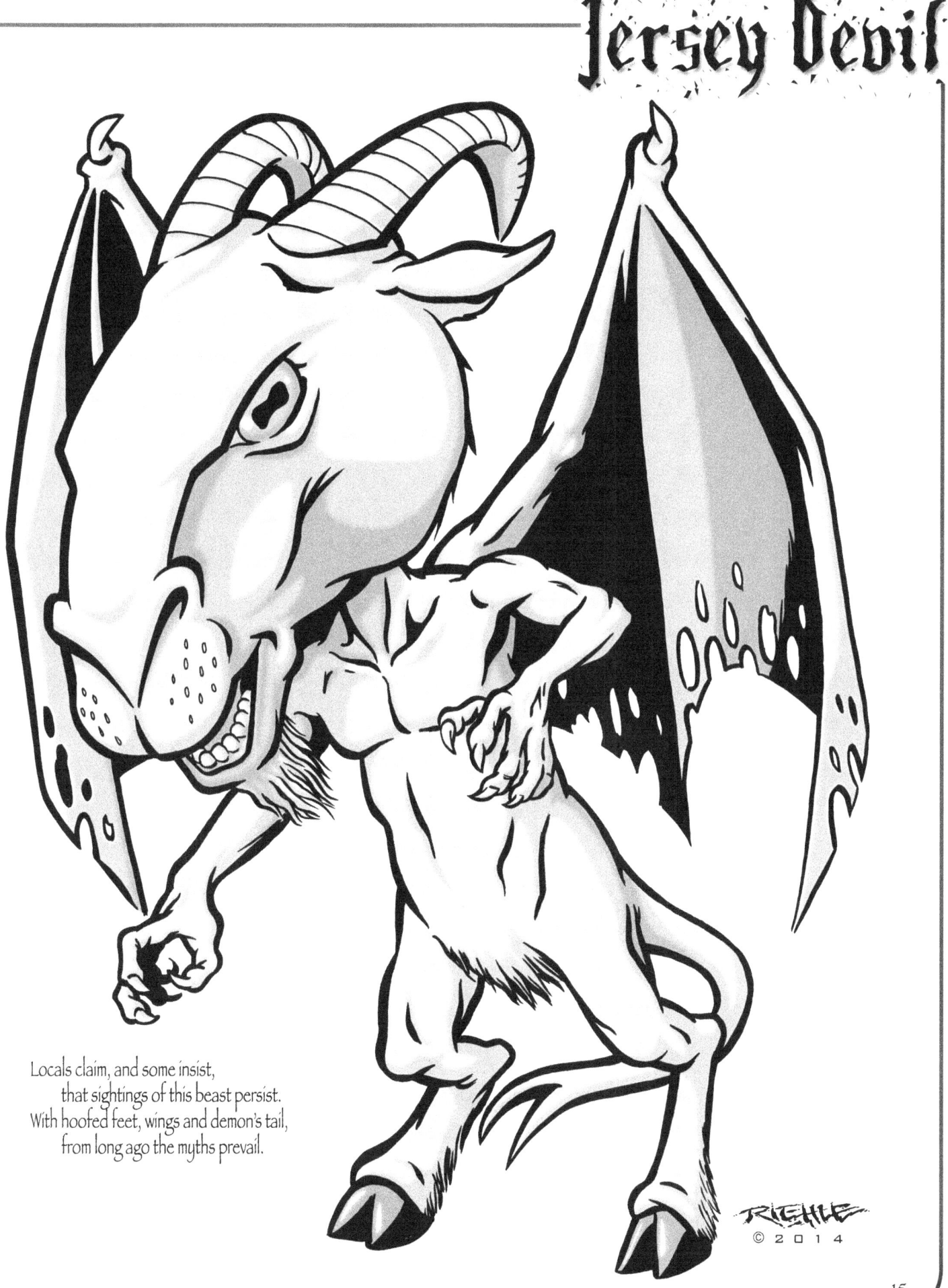

Locals claim, and some insist,
that sightings of this beast persist.
With hoofed feet, wings and demon's tail,
from long ago the myths prevail.

RIEHLE
© 2 0 1 4

Giant

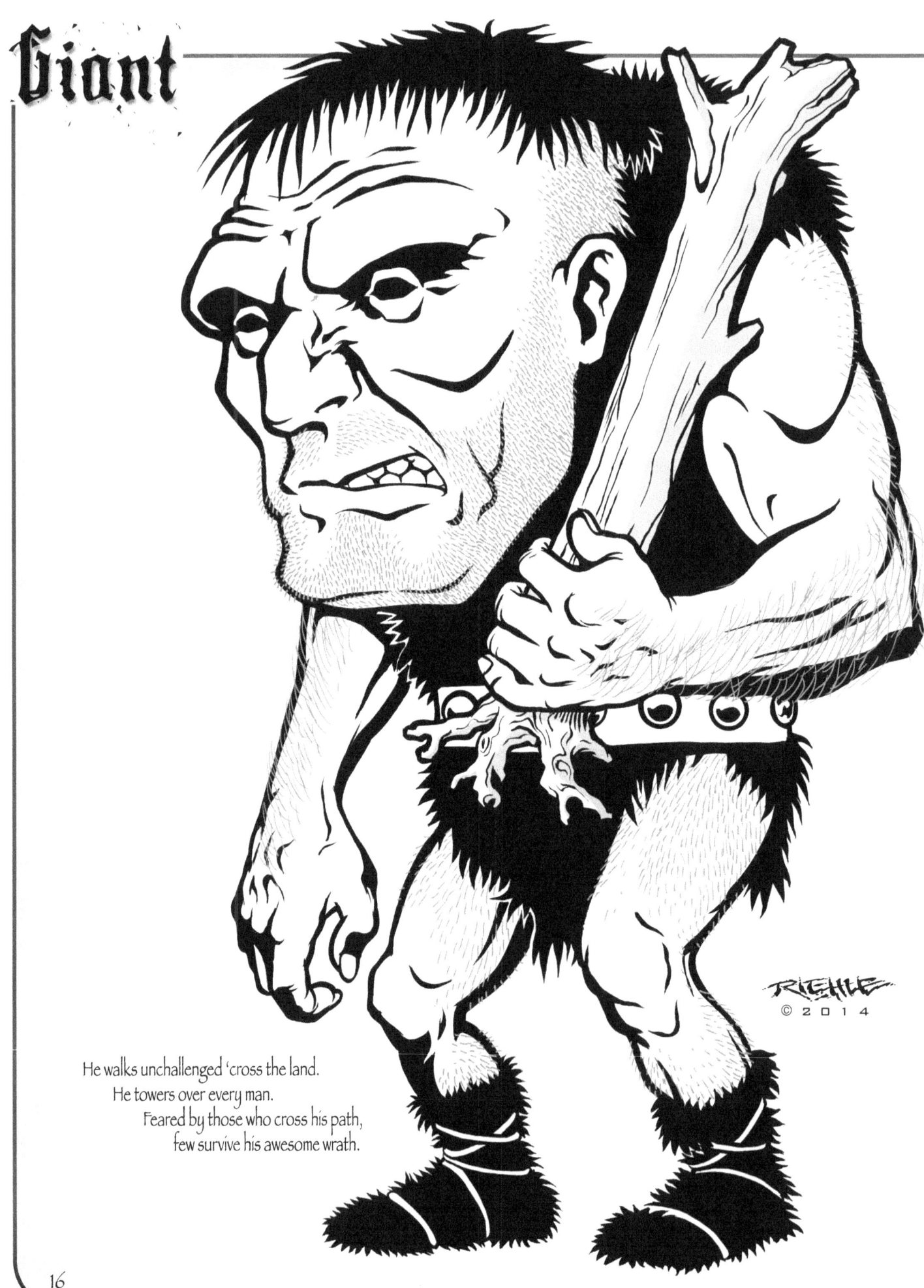

He walks unchallenged 'cross the land.
He towers over every man.
Feared by those who cross his path,
few survive his awesome wrath.

Minotaur

A horror born part man, part bull,
two things apart now one made full.
Into the labyrinth he's cast,
lost then in a maze so vast.

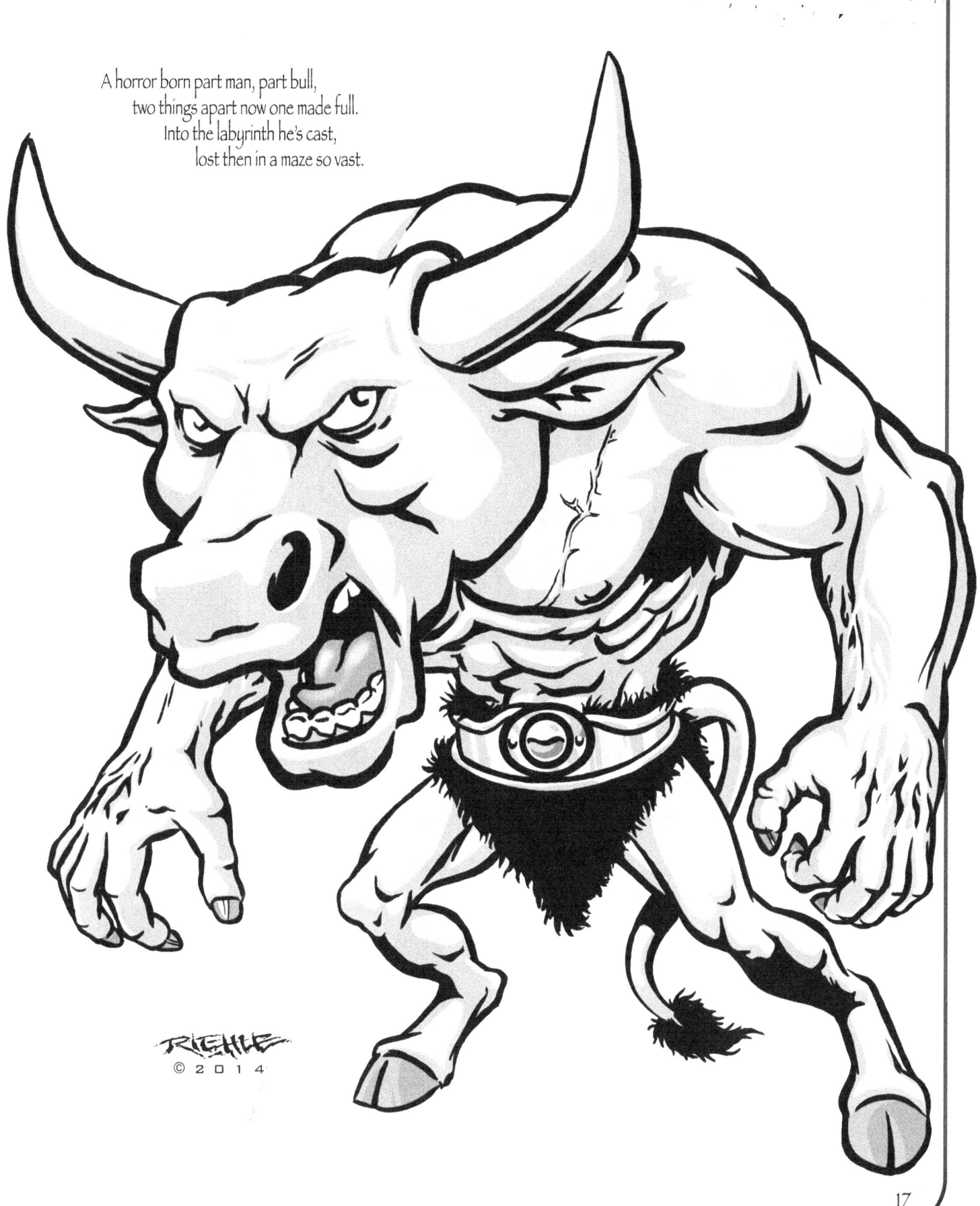

Gremlin

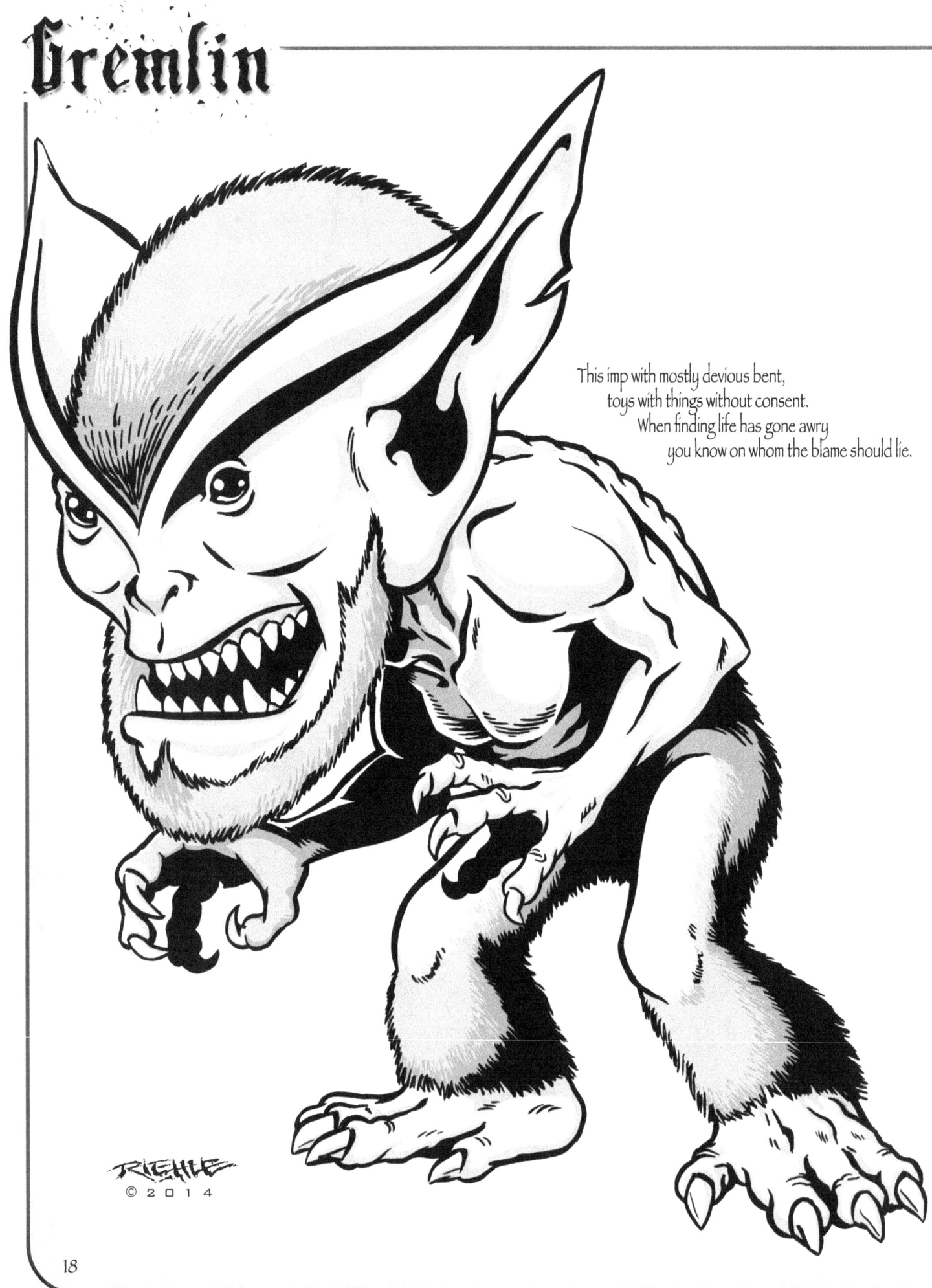

This imp with mostly devious bent,
toys with things without consent.
When finding life has gone awry
you know on whom the blame should lie.

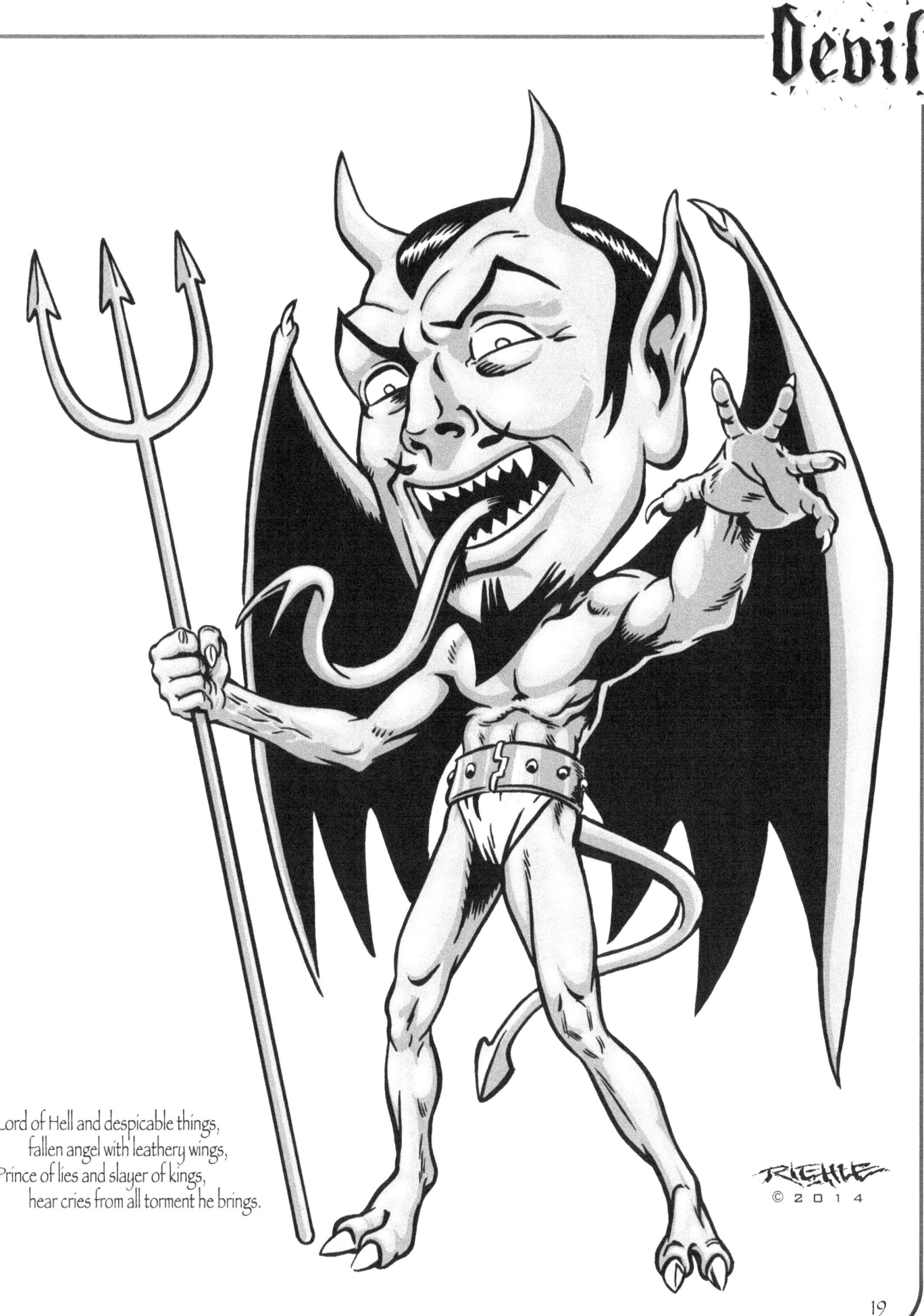

Lord of Hell and despicable things,
   fallen angel with leathery wings,
Prince of lies and slayer of kings,
   hear cries from all torment he brings.

RIEHLE
© 2 0 1 4

Banshee

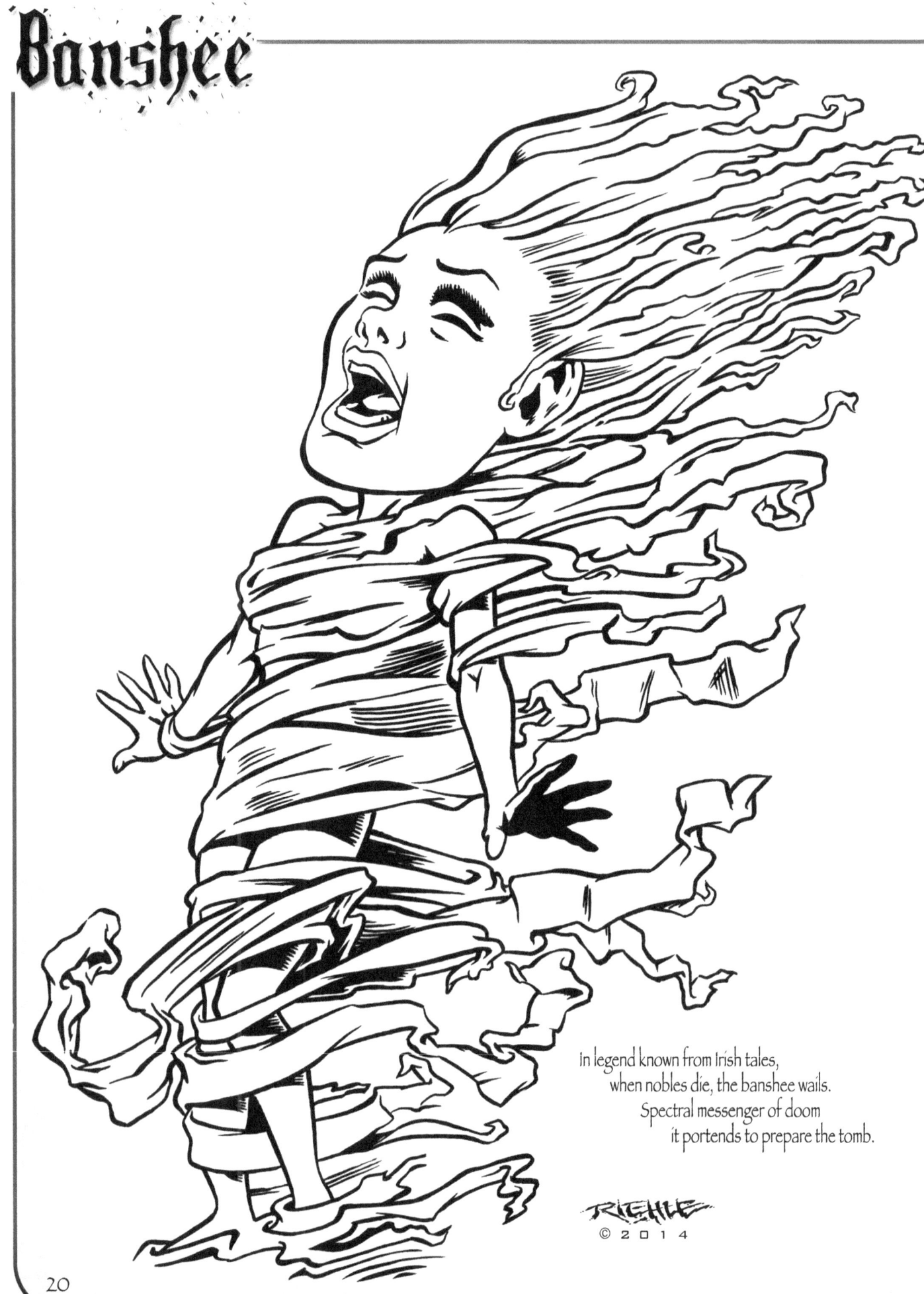

In legend known from Irish tales,
when nobles die, the banshee wails.
Spectral messenger of doom
it portends to prepare the tomb.

RICHLE
© 2014

Chupacabra

Beware the night, for while we sleep,
it drinks the blood of goats and sheep.
Concealed from view it's rarely seen,
known mostly from its deeds; unclean.

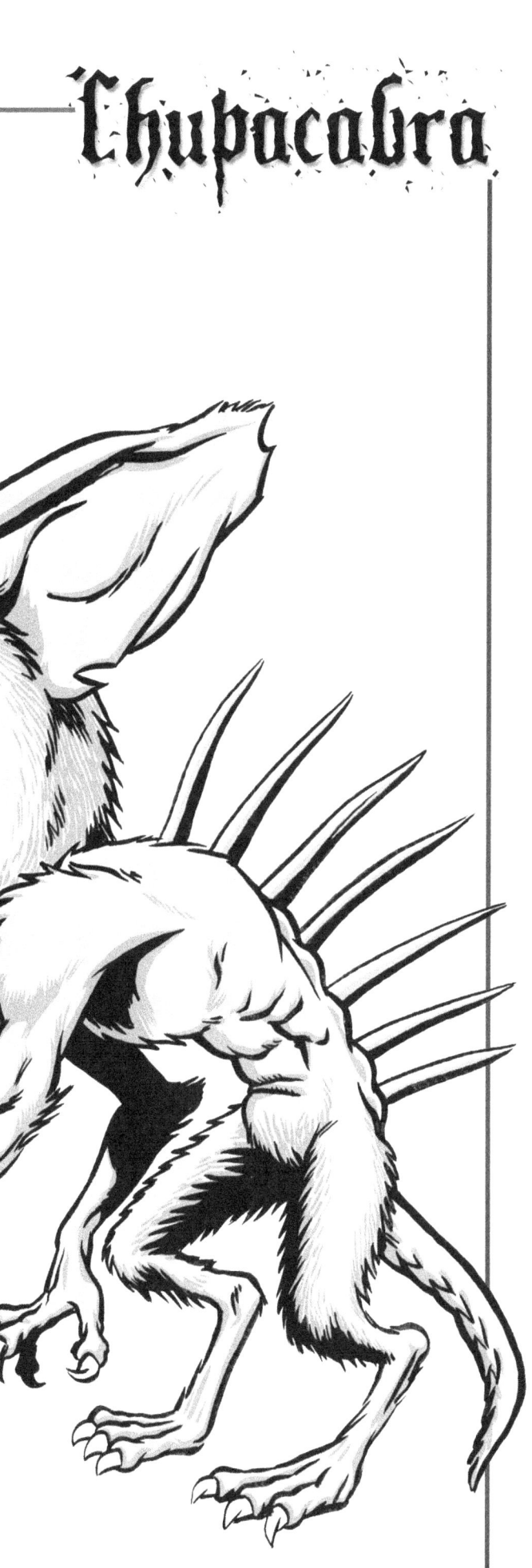

RIEHLE
© 2 0 1 4

Satyr

Deep in forest shade and cover,
he plays his pipes to lure a lover.
Child of nature, gentle faun,
enjoying life from dusk 'til dawn.

RIEHLE
© 2 0 1 4

Invisible Man

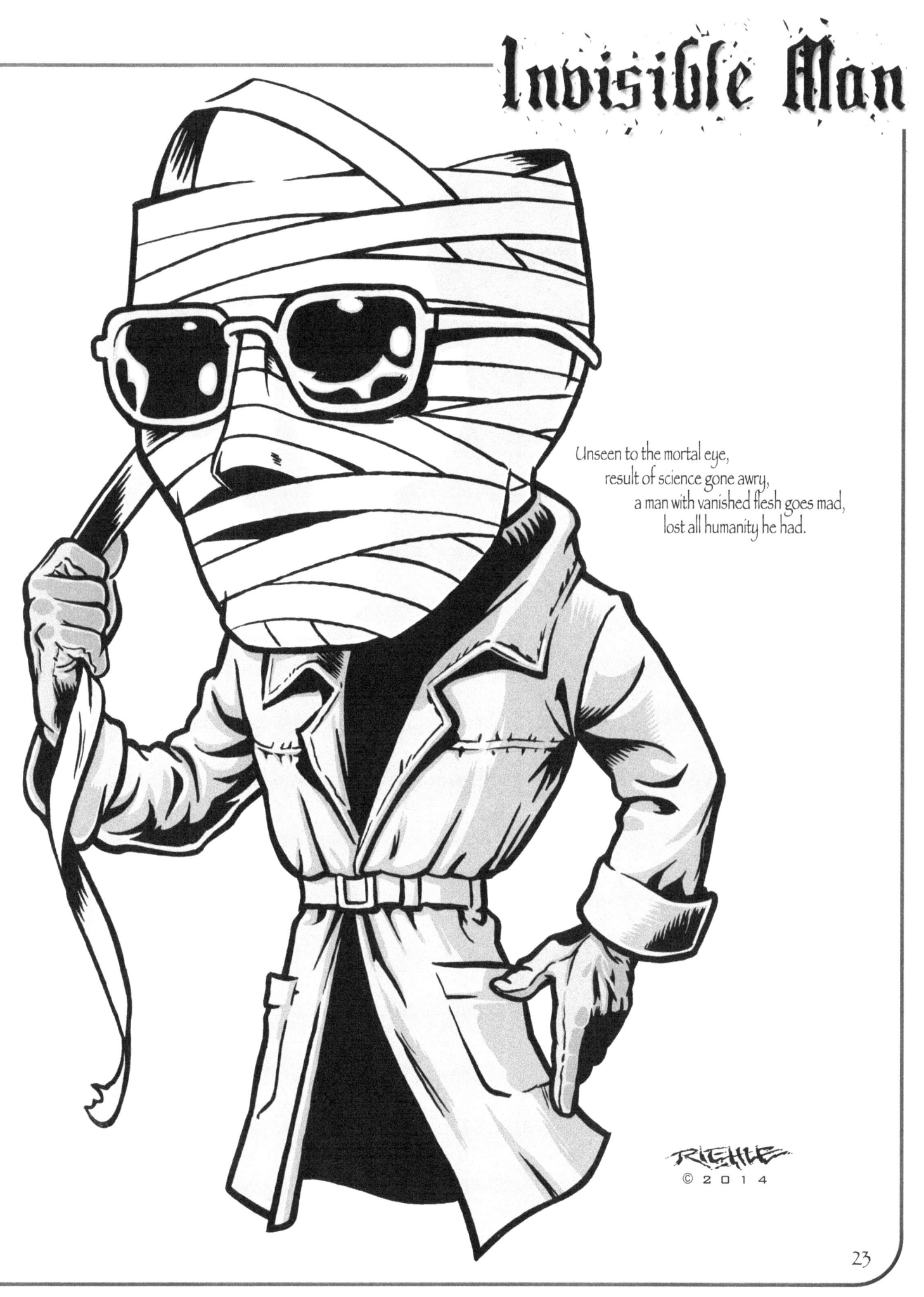

Unseen to the mortal eye,
result of science gone awry,
a man with vanished flesh goes mad,
lost all humanity he had.

RICHLE
© 2 0 1 4

Harpy

The Greeks knew well this bird from Hell
would torment men when hard times fell.
With talons sharp and broad of wing,
the wary shun this ghastly thing.

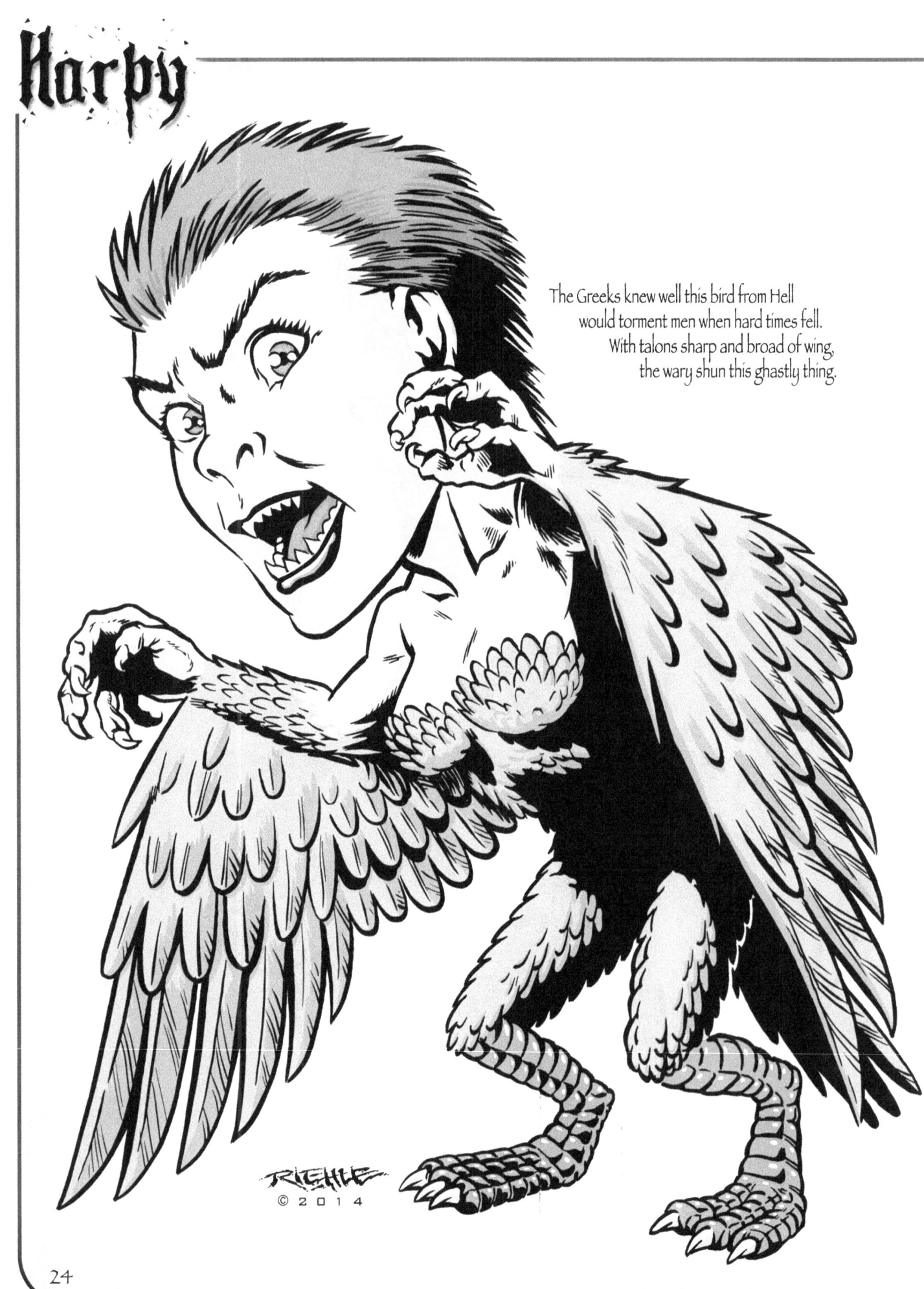

Morlock

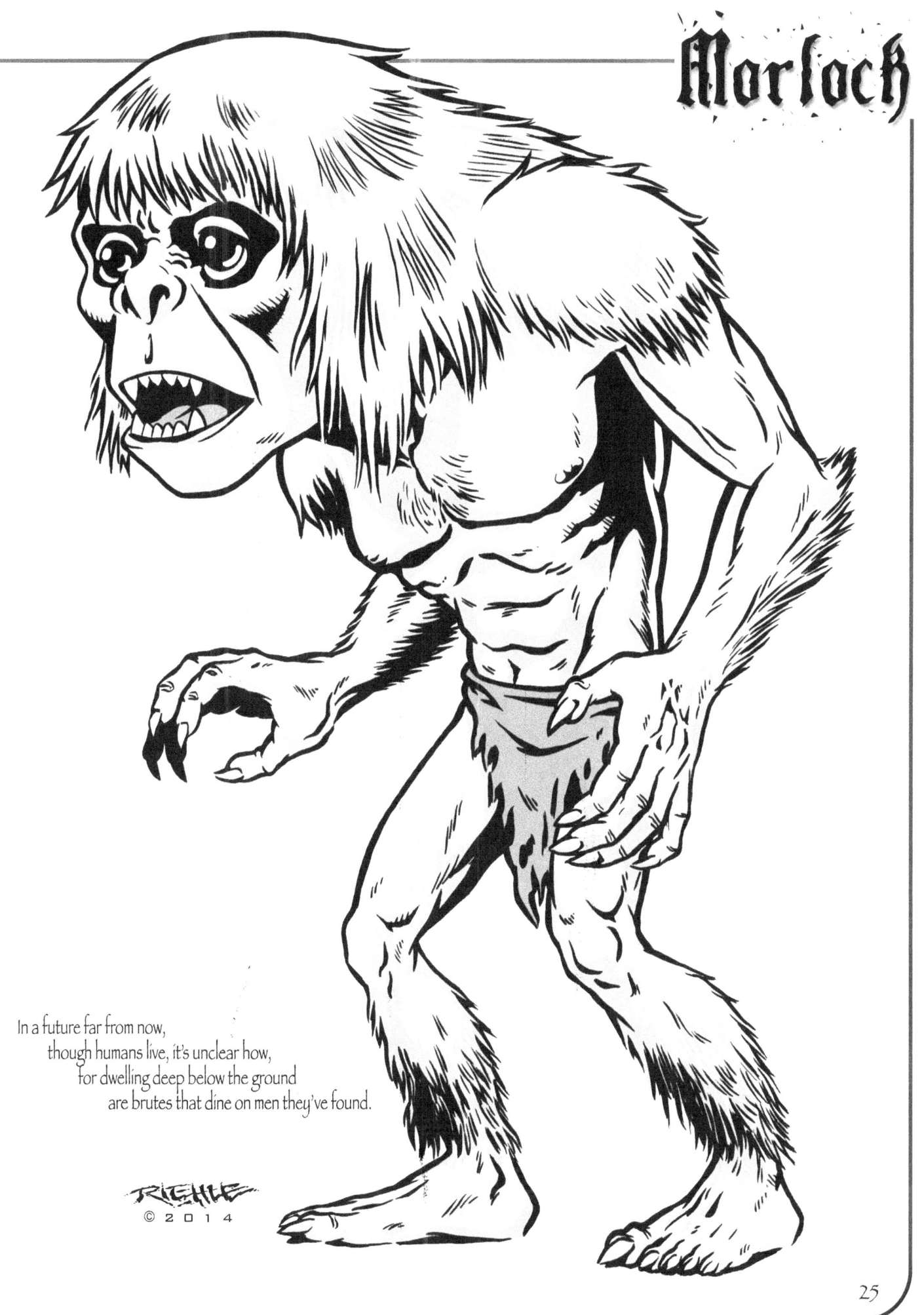

In a future far from now,
though humans live, it's unclear how,
for dwelling deep below the ground
are brutes that dine on men they've found.

RIEHLE
© 2 0 1 4

25

Vampire

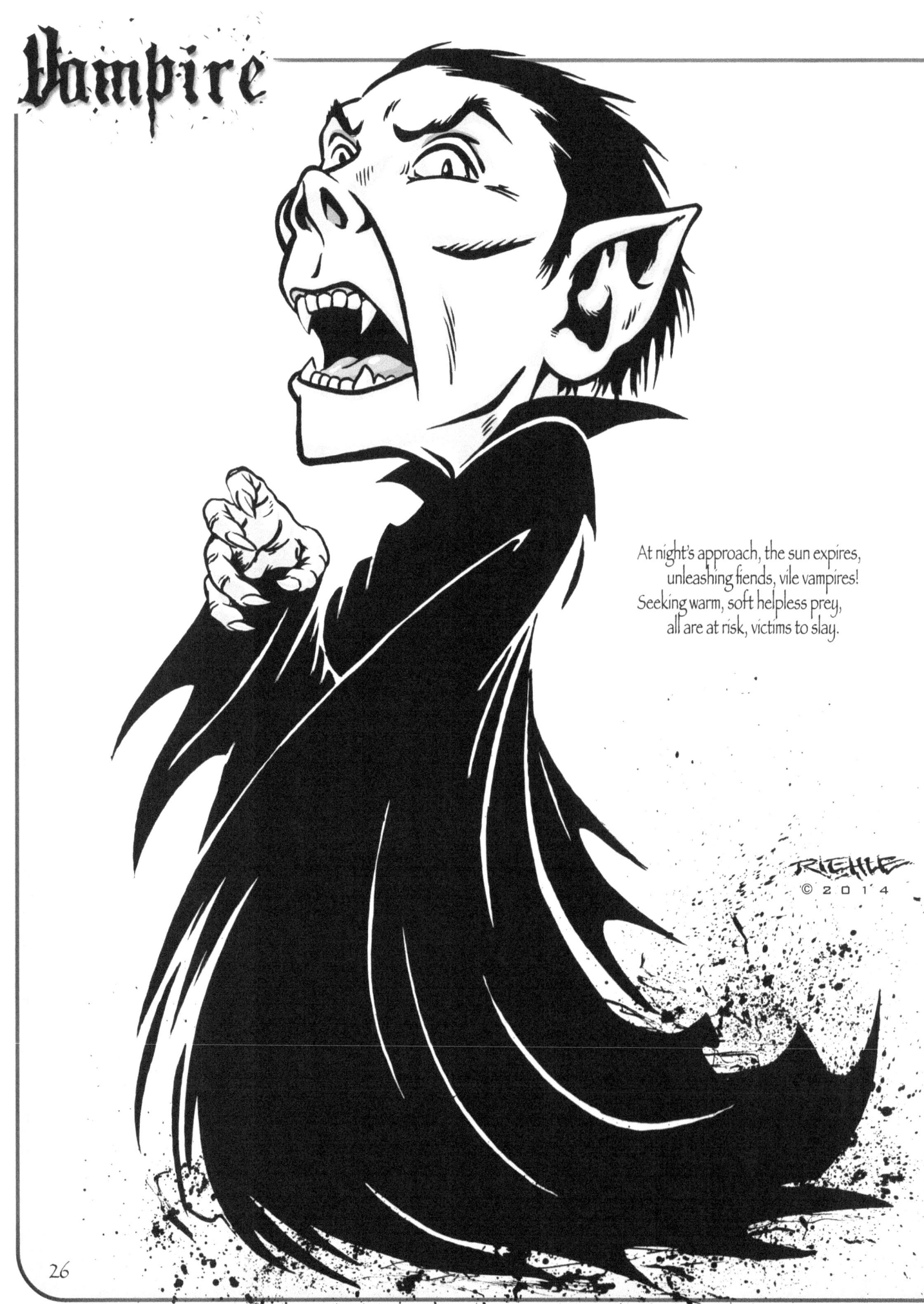

At night's approach, the sun expires,
unleashing fiends, vile vampires!
Seeking warm, soft helpless prey,
all are at risk, victims to slay.

RIEHLE
© 2 0 1 4

Zombie

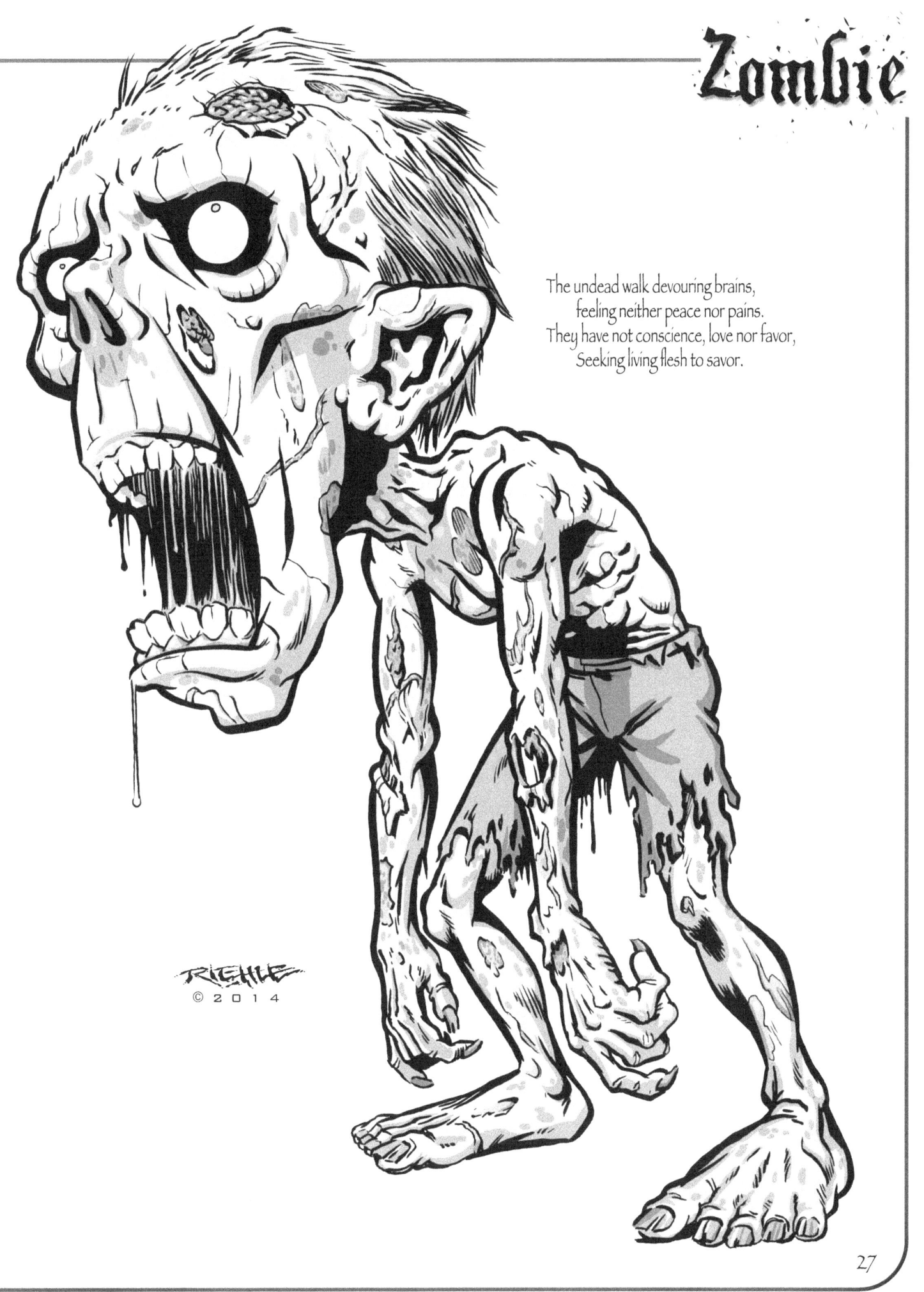

The undead walk devouring brains,
feeling neither peace nor pains.
They have not conscience, love nor favor,
Seeking living flesh to savor.

RIEHLE
© 2 0 1 4

Troll

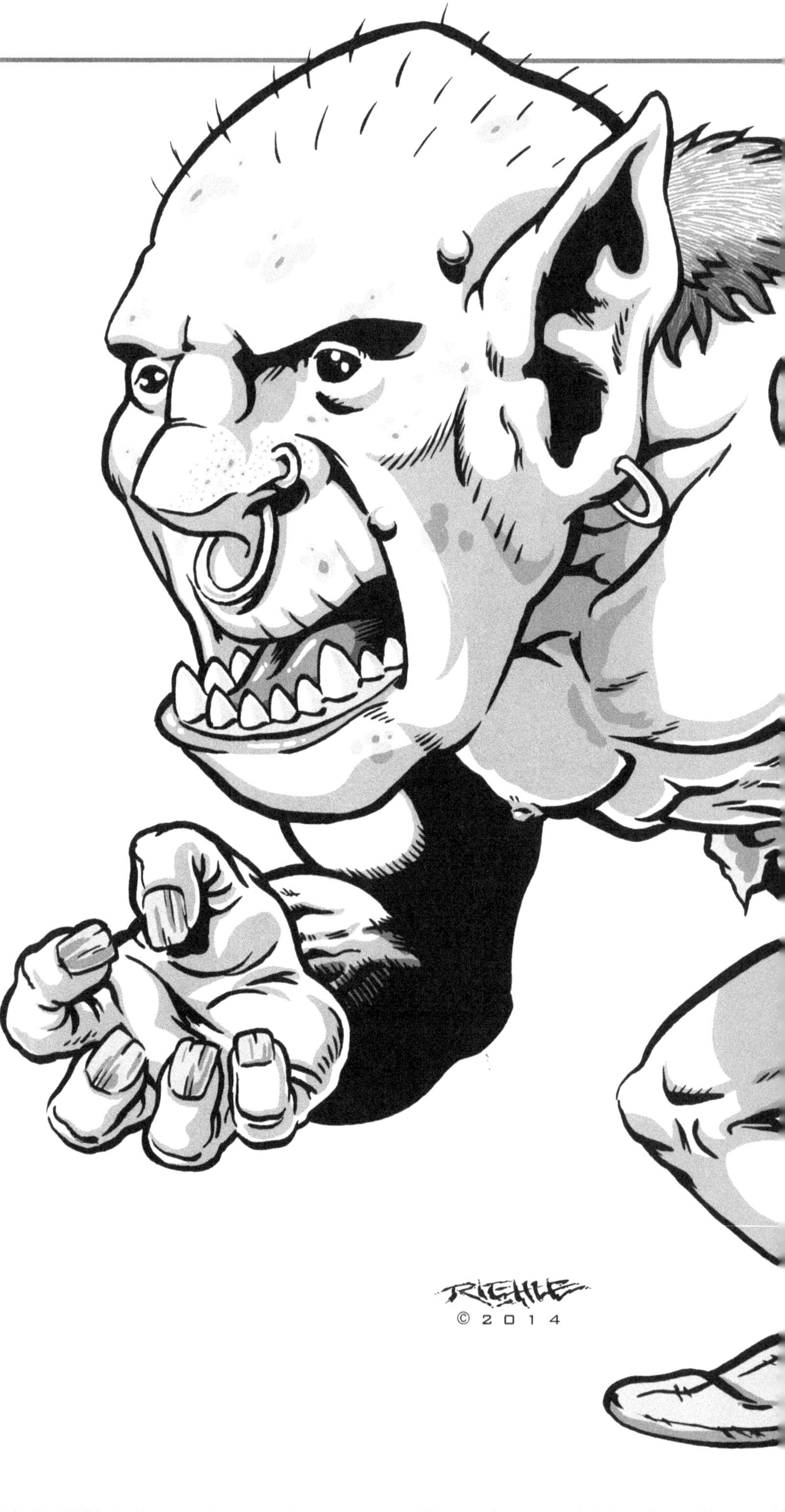

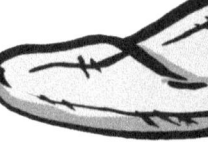

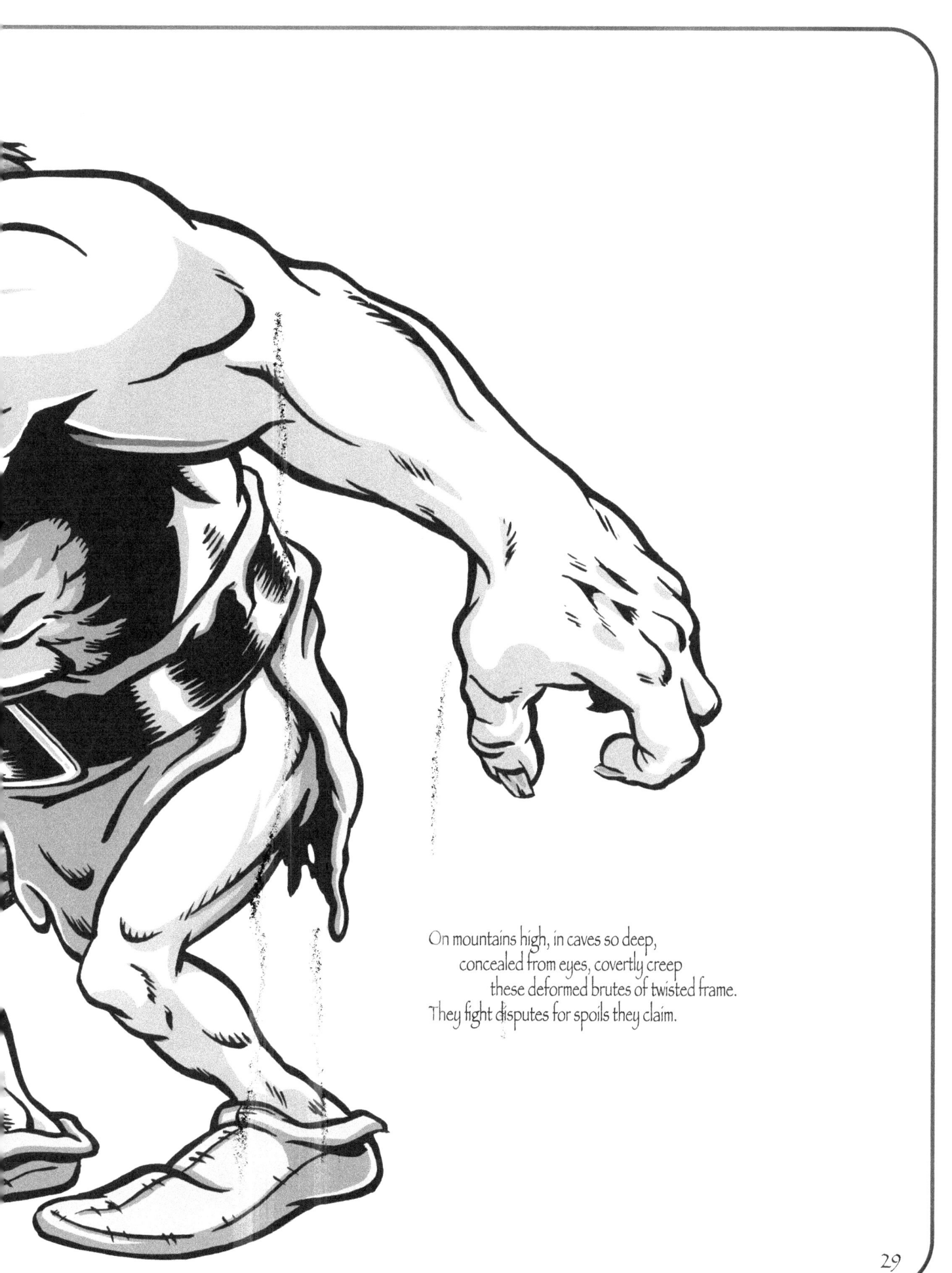

On mountains high, in caves so deep,
concealed from eyes, covertly creep
these deformed brutes of twisted frame.
They fight disputes for spoils they claim.

Ghoul

A stranger smiles a twisted face,
trespassing final resting place.
He lurks in gloom behind the graves,
to search for human flesh he craves.

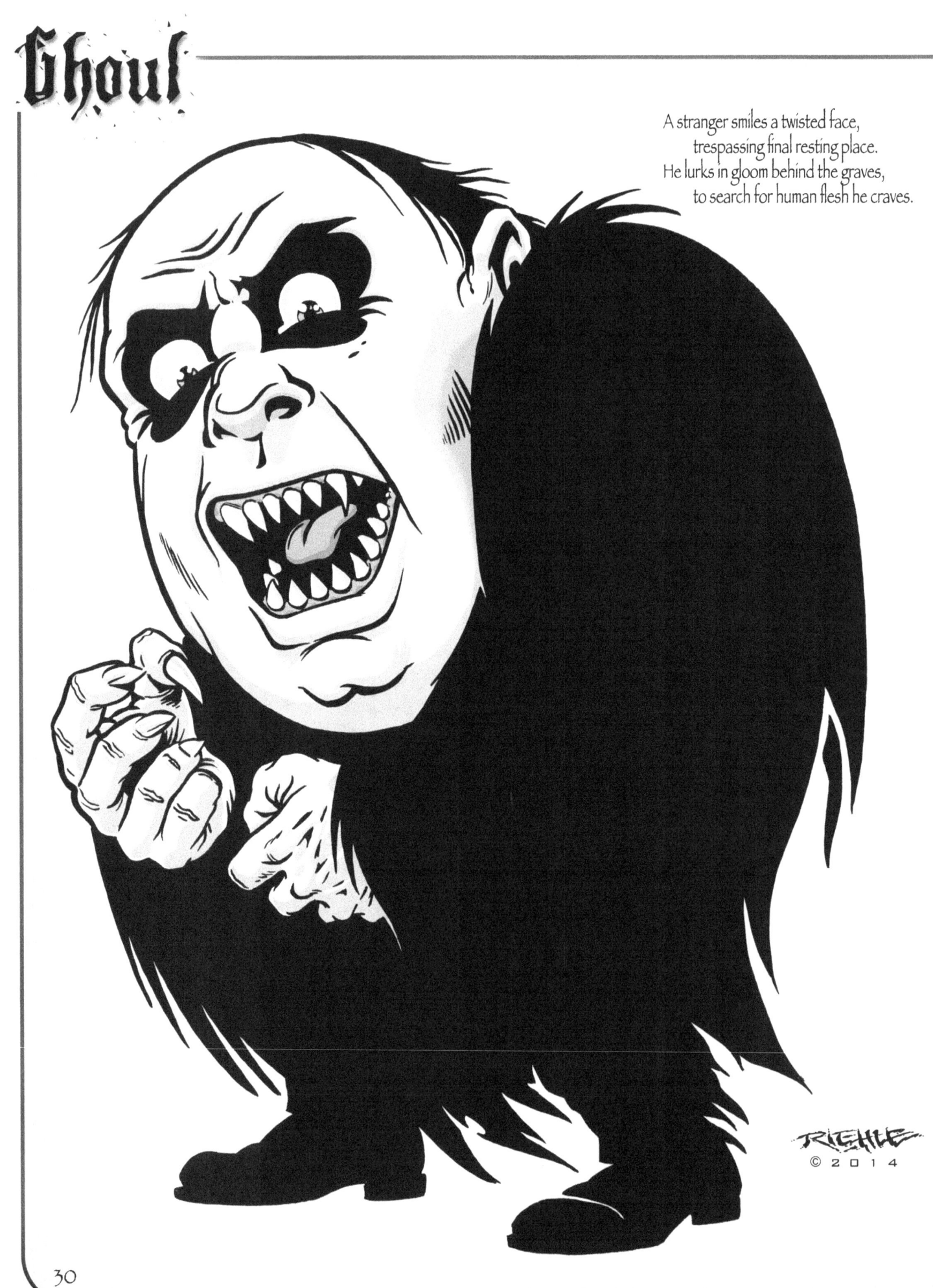

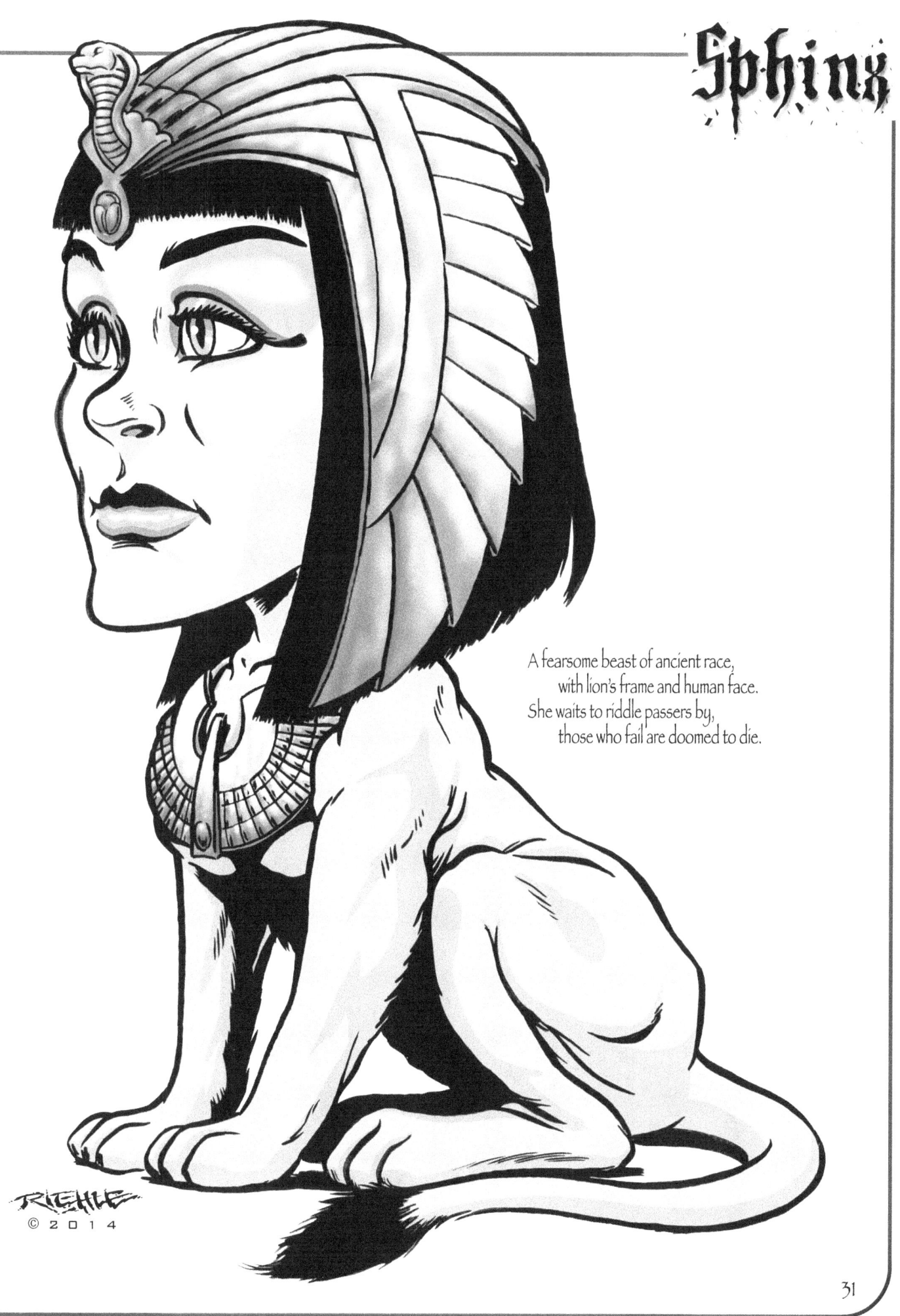

Sphinx

A fearsome beast of ancient race,
 with lion's frame and human face.
She waits to riddle passers by,
 those who fail are doomed to die.

RIEHLE
© 2014

Cerberus

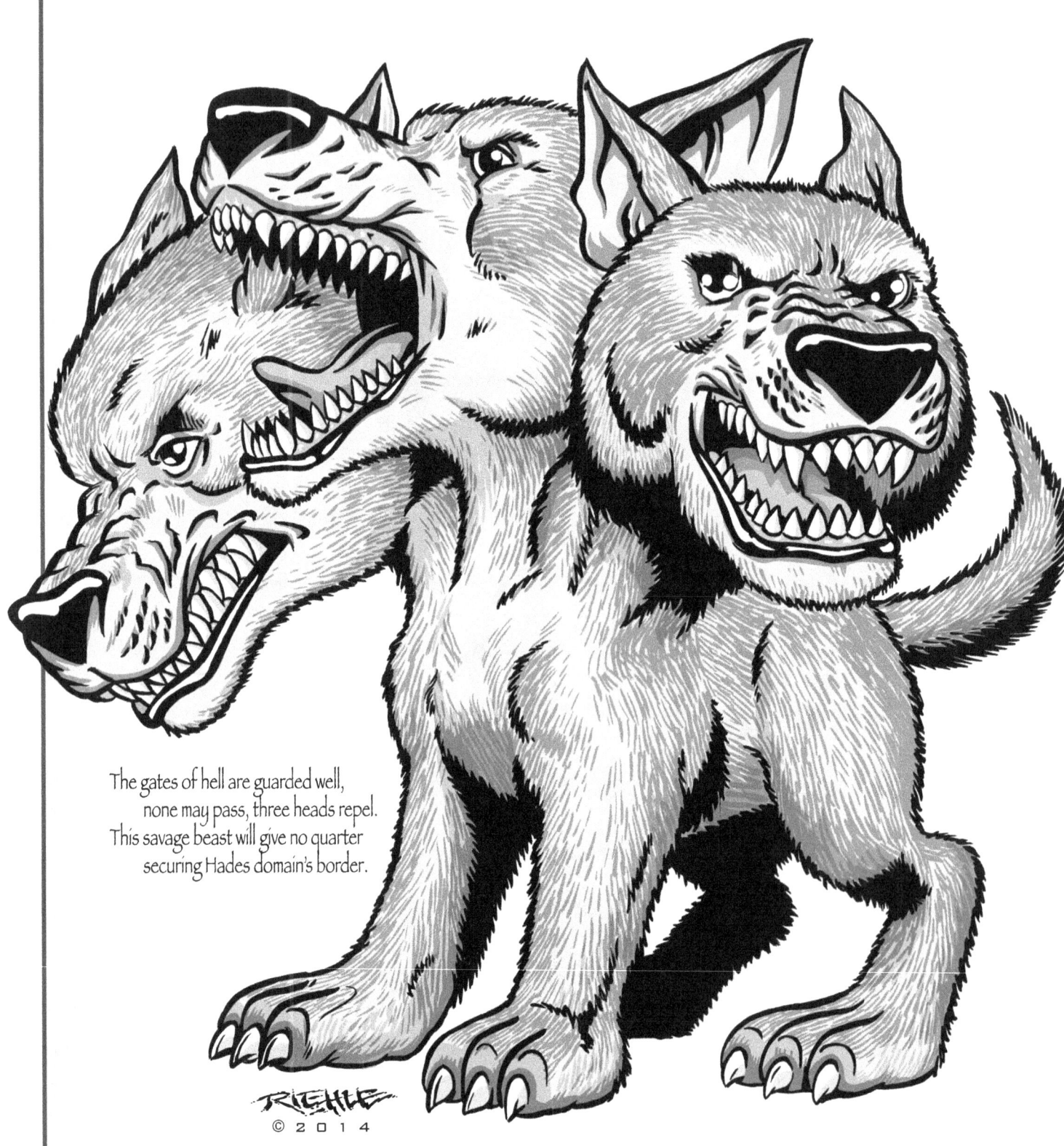

The gates of hell are guarded well,
none may pass, three heads repel.
This savage beast will give no quarter
securing Hades domain's border.

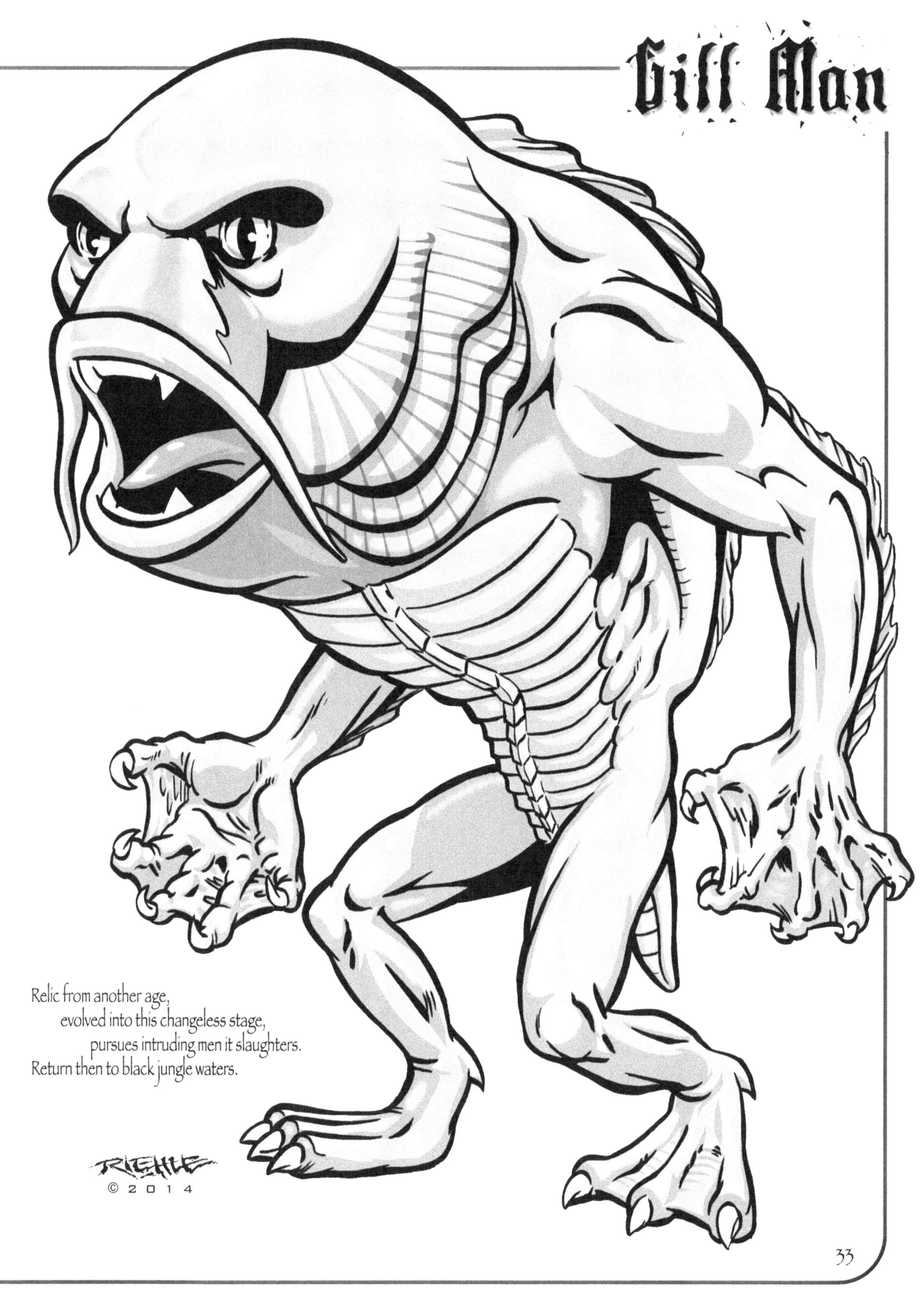

Gill Man

Relic from another age,
    evolved into this changeless stage,
        pursues intruding men it slaughters.
Return then to black jungle waters.

RICHLE
© 2 0 1 4

33

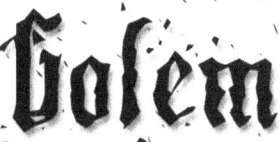

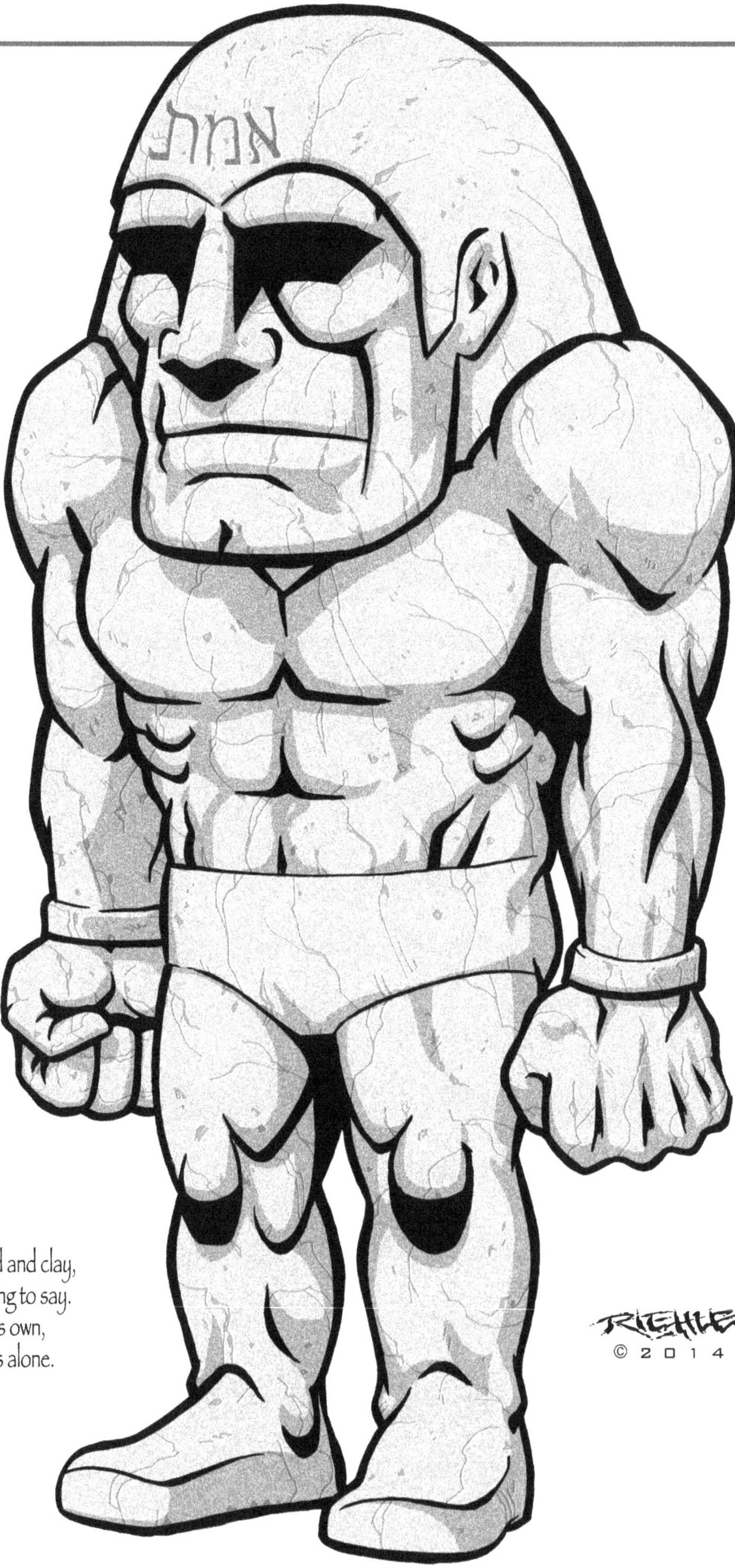

A creature forged of mud and clay,
mute of voice, nothing to say.
A soulless slave, no will its own,
called to life, it walks alone.

RIEHLE
© 2014

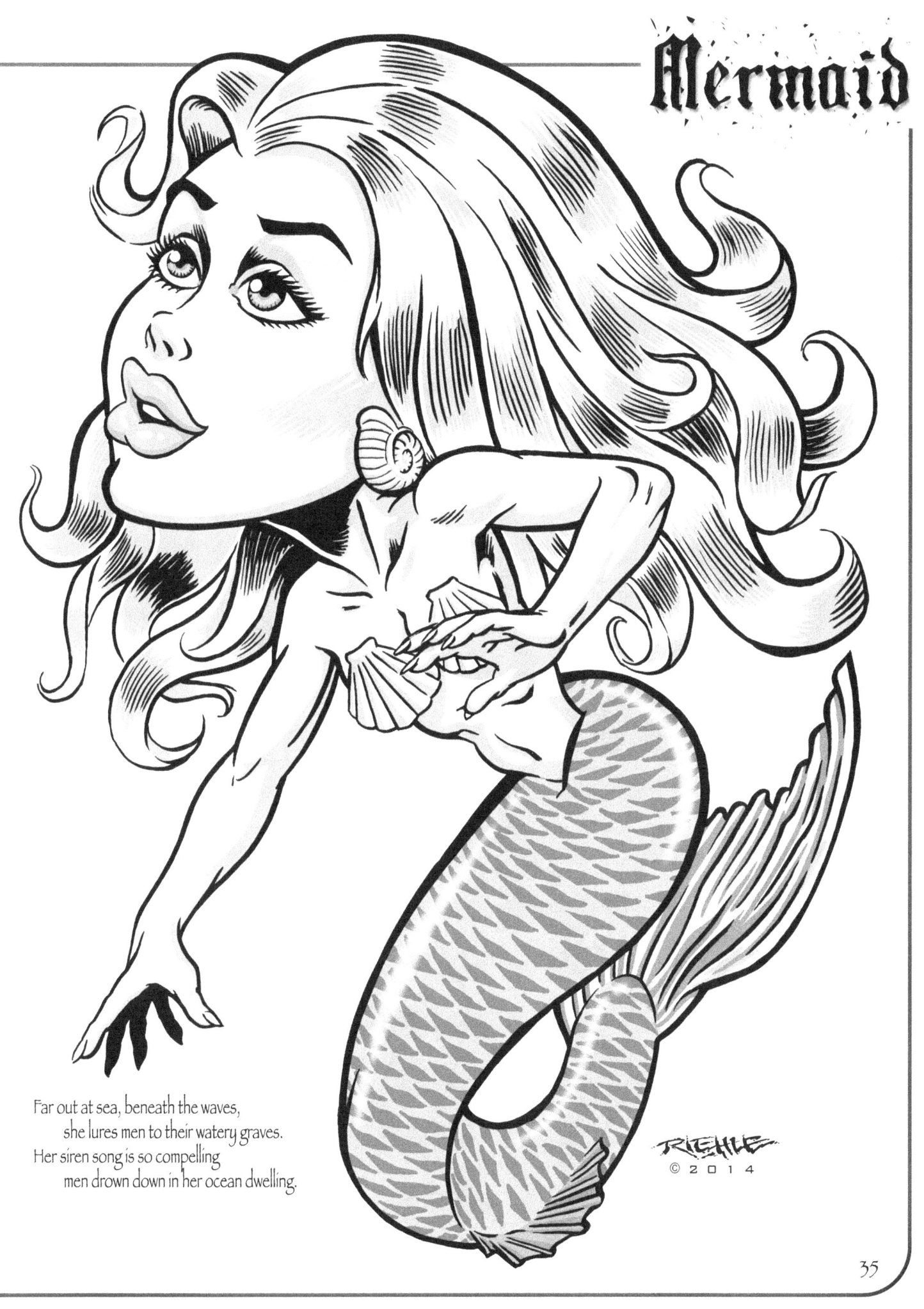

Mermaid

Far out at sea, beneath the waves,
   she lures men to their watery graves.
Her siren song is so compelling
   men drown down in her ocean dwelling.

RIEHLE
© 2014

Medusa

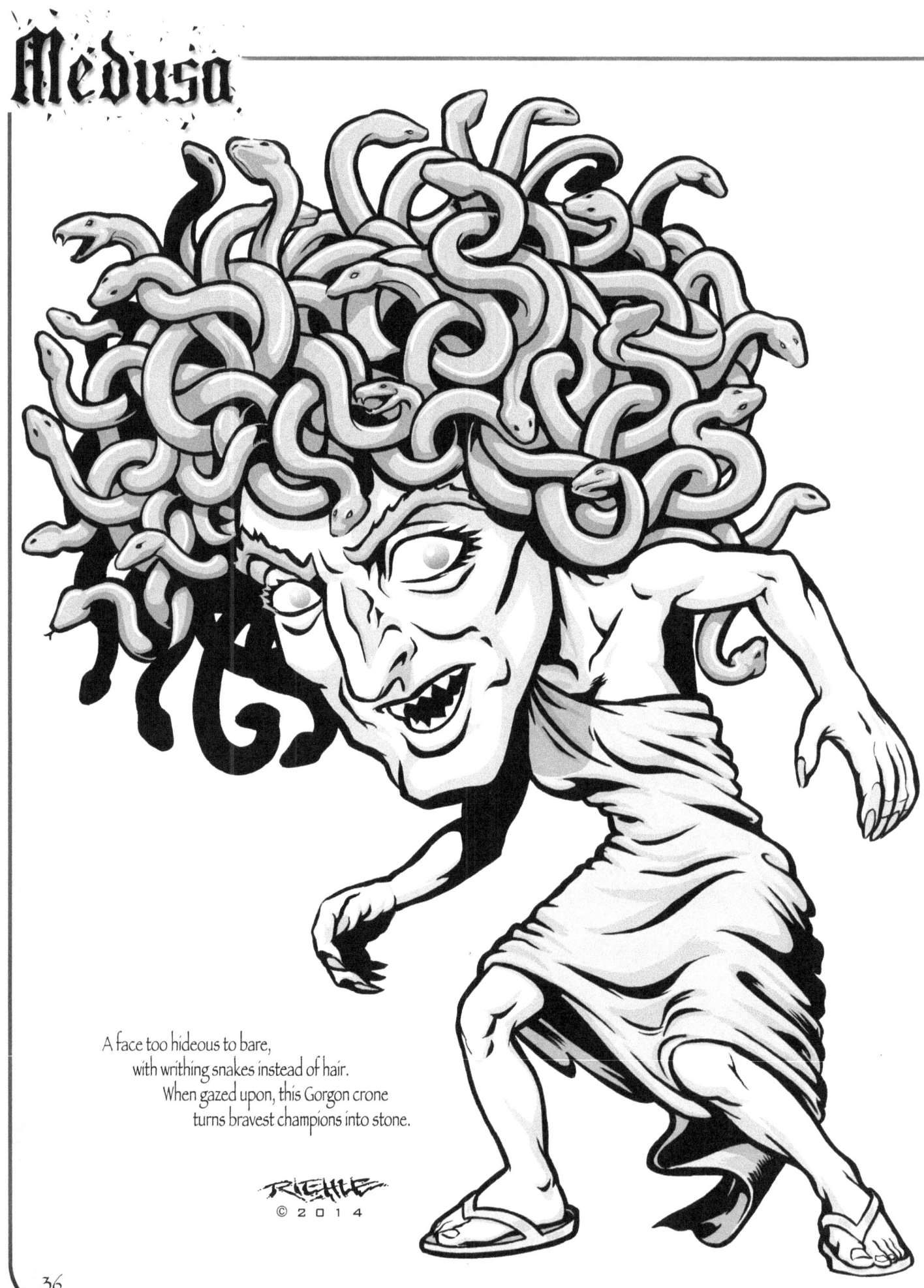

A face too hideous to bare,
with writhing snakes instead of hair.
When gazed upon, this Gorgon crone
turns bravest champions into stone.

RIEHLE
© 2 0 1 4

Frankenstein Monster

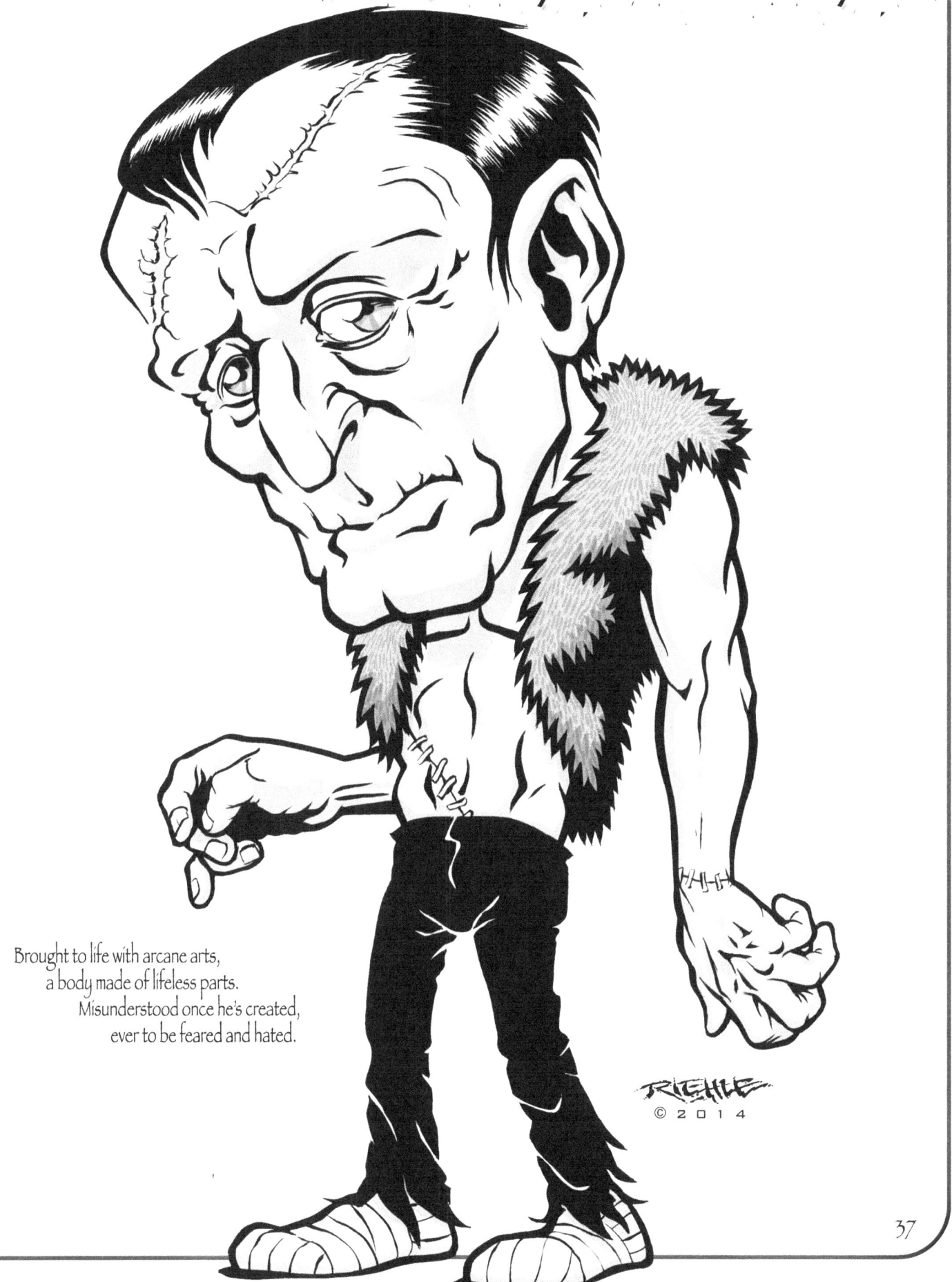

Brought to life with arcane arts,
a body made of lifeless parts.
Misunderstood once he's created,
ever to be feared and hated.

RIEHLE
© 2014

Cyborg

In times to come when science splices
humans with high tech devices,
a race of beings will arise
to leave behind the mortal guise.

RIEHLE
© 2 0 1 4

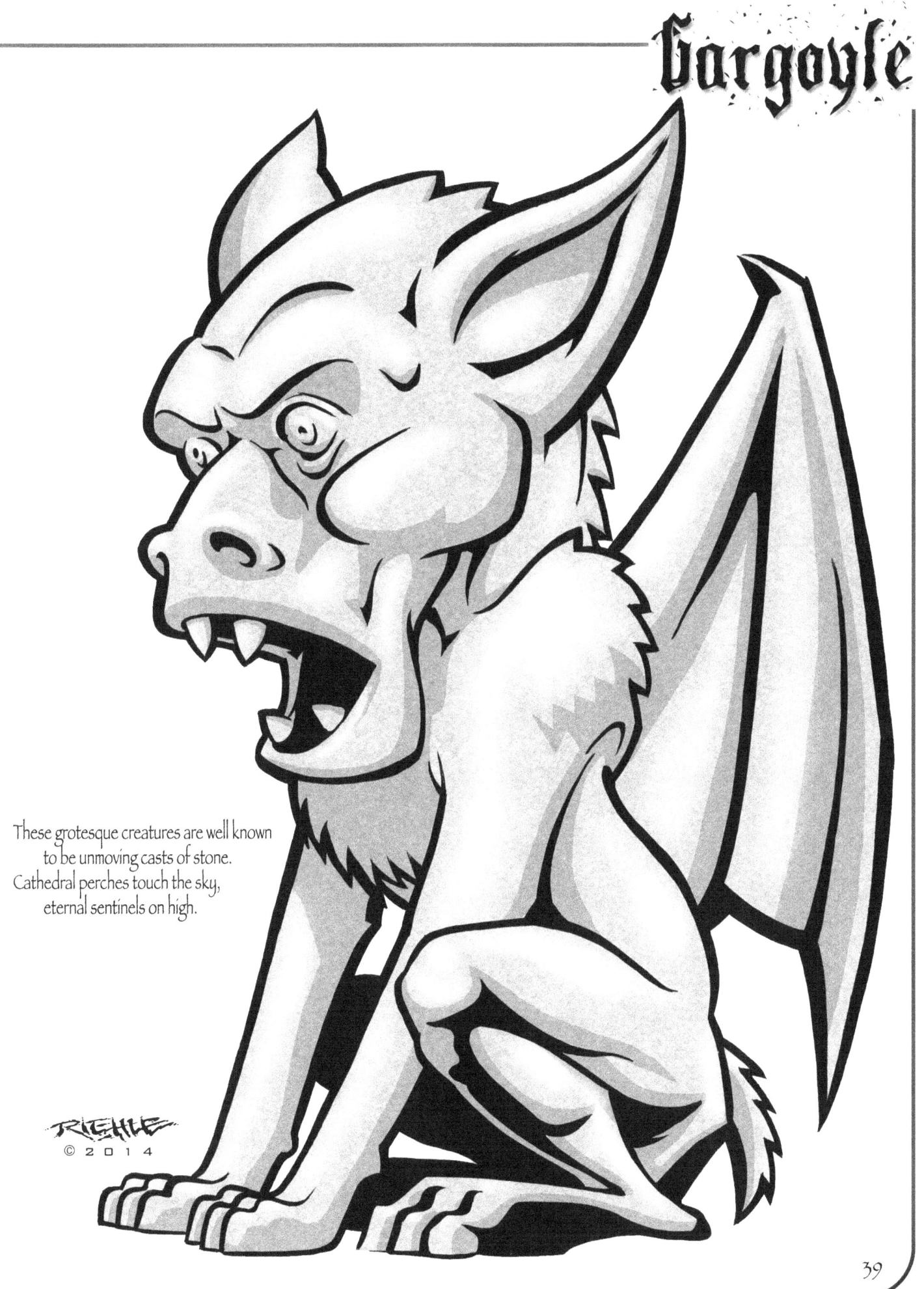

These grotesque creatures are well known
to be unmoving casts of stone.
Cathedral perches touch the sky,
eternal sentinels on high.

RIEHLE
© 2 0 1 4

Lake Monster

Tales told of the loch so deep
a creature in the depths does sleep.
Infrequently to surface rise
and catch onlookers by surprise.

RICHLE
© 2 0 1 4

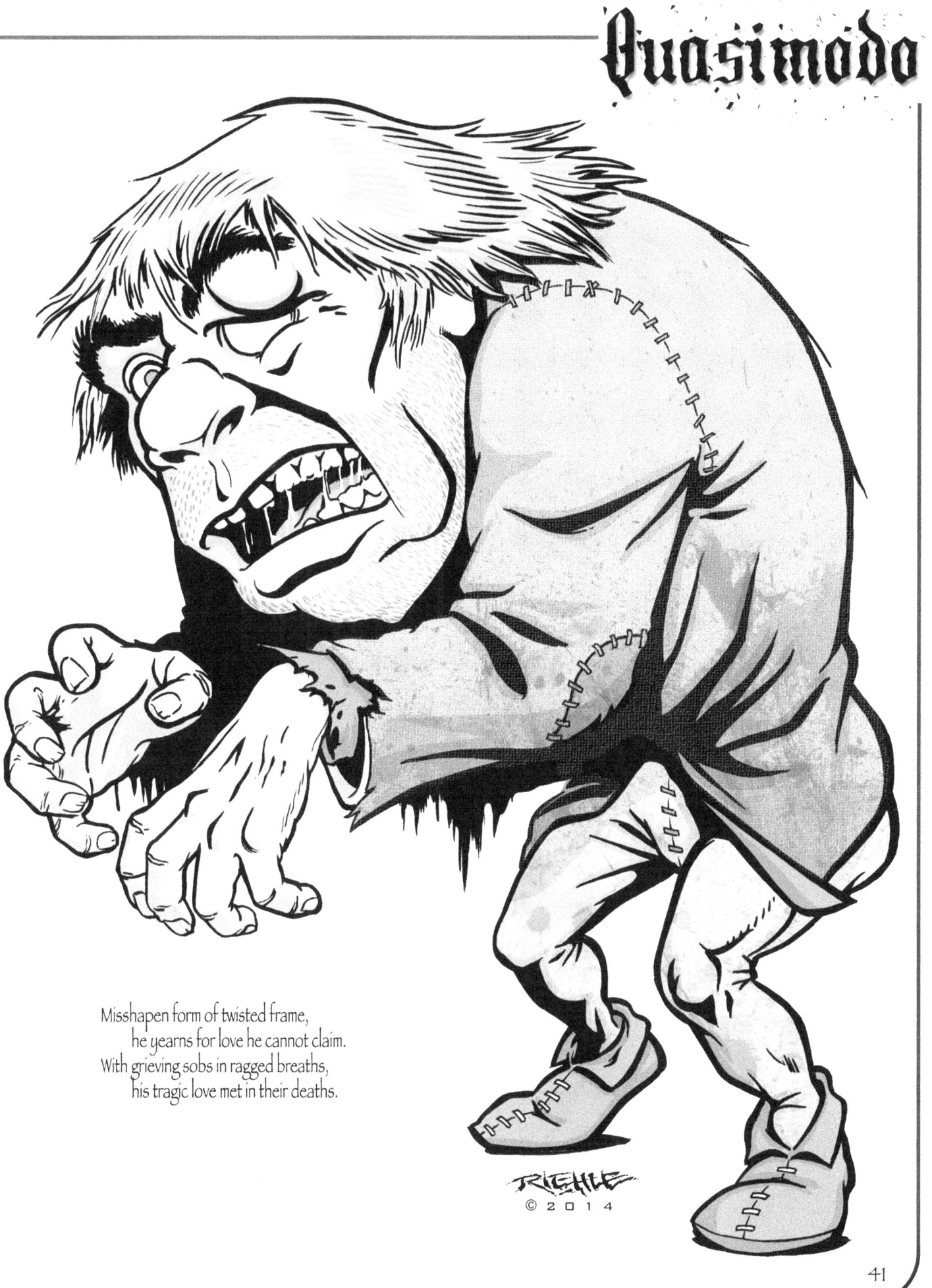

Quasimodo

Misshapen form of twisted frame,
     he yearns for love he cannot claim.
With grieving sobs in ragged breaths,
     his tragic love met in their deaths.

RIEHLE
© 2 0 1 4

Moth Man

It soars on wings of prophesy
enshrouded in dark mystery.
When seen, an omen to behold
warns tragic events to unfold.

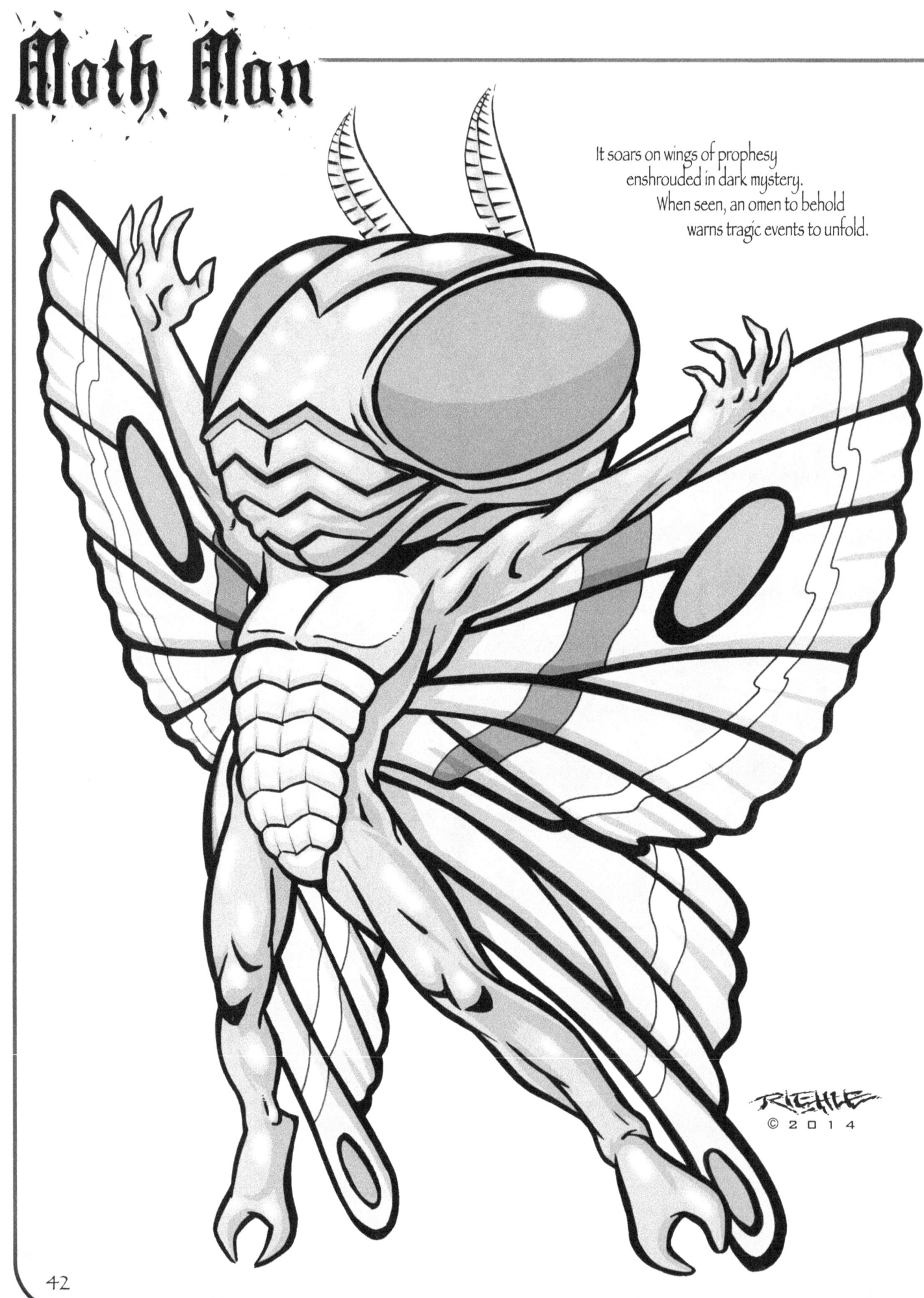

RIEHLE
© 2 0 1 4

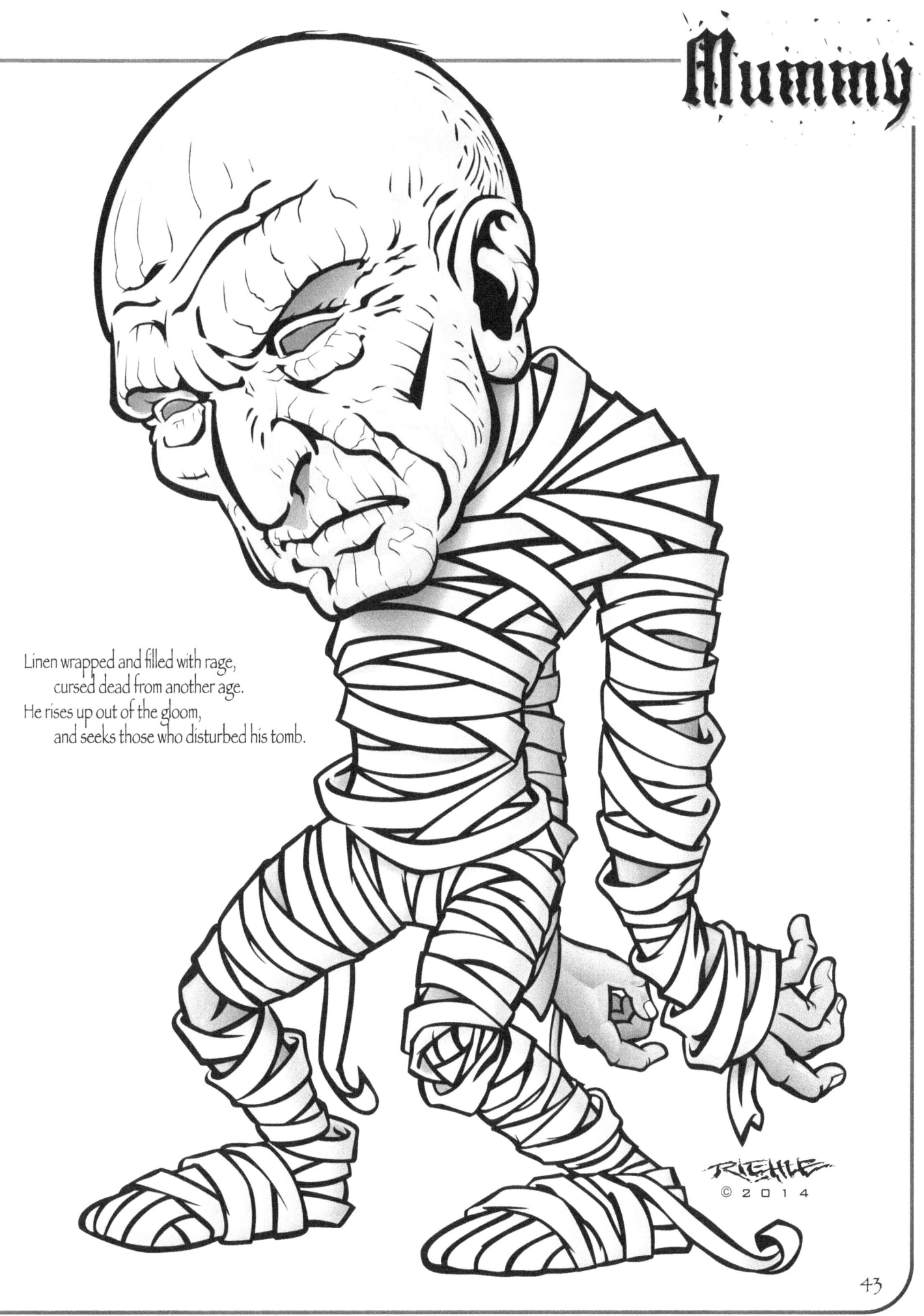

Mummy

Linen wrapped and filled with rage,
    cursed dead from another age.
He rises up out of the gloom,
    and seeks those who disturbed his tomb.

RIEHLE
© 2014

43

RoBot

Circuits, wires, in metal case,
a slave to serve the human race.
Technology, evolving faster,
may turn the slave into the master.

RIEHLE
© 2014

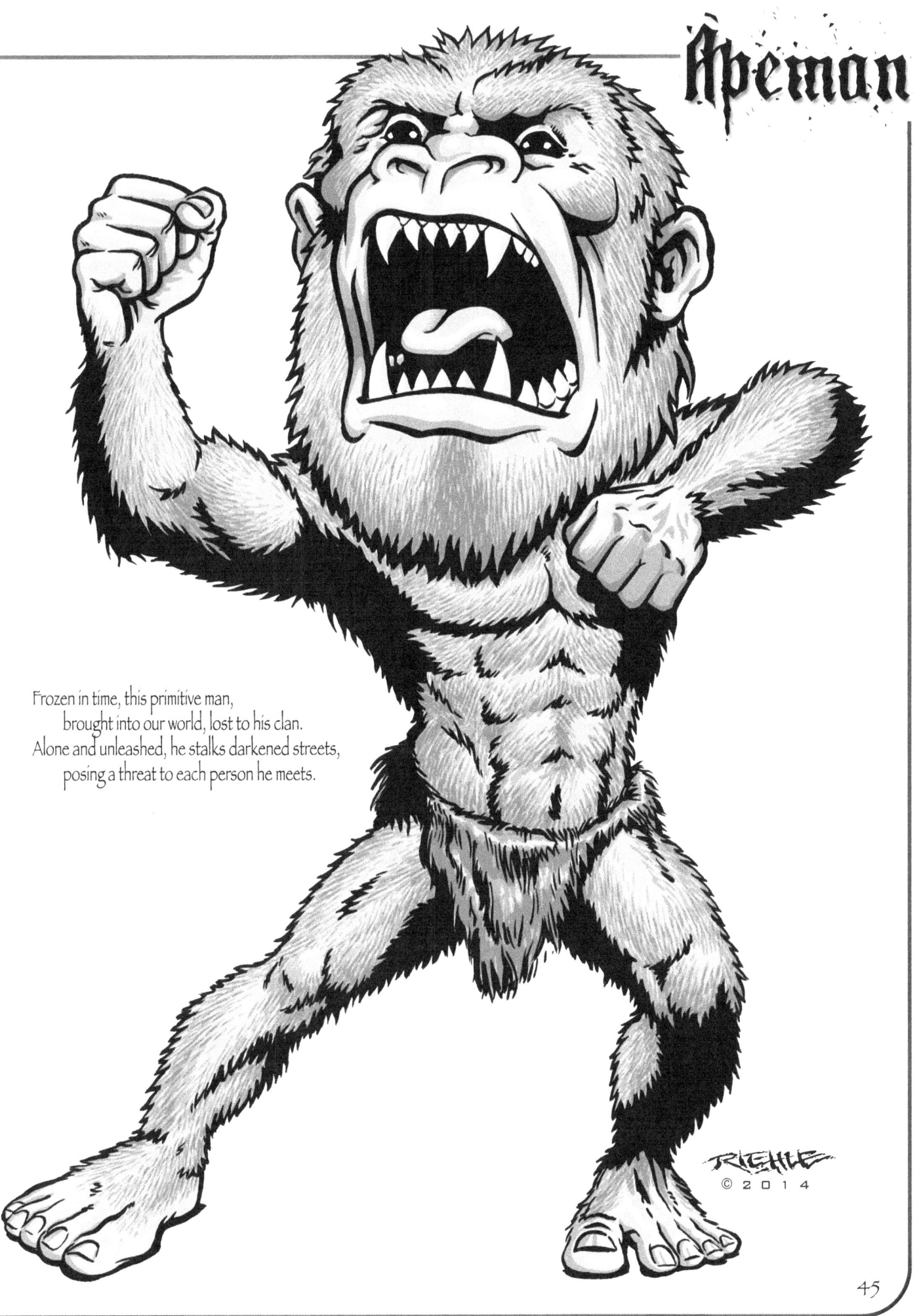

Apeman

Frozen in time, this primitive man,
brought into our world, lost to his clan.
Alone and unleashed, he stalks darkened streets,
posing a threat to each person he meets.

RIEHLE
© 2 0 1 4

Dragon

Steely scales and teeth like daggers,
from nightmares formed, fearless it swaggers
to challenge those, the brave of heart,
whose bloody bones it rips apart.

Witch

Spirits high on Halloween,
   up in the sky, you swear you've seen
    fly 'cross the moon, a witch on broom!
   Hallucination you presume.

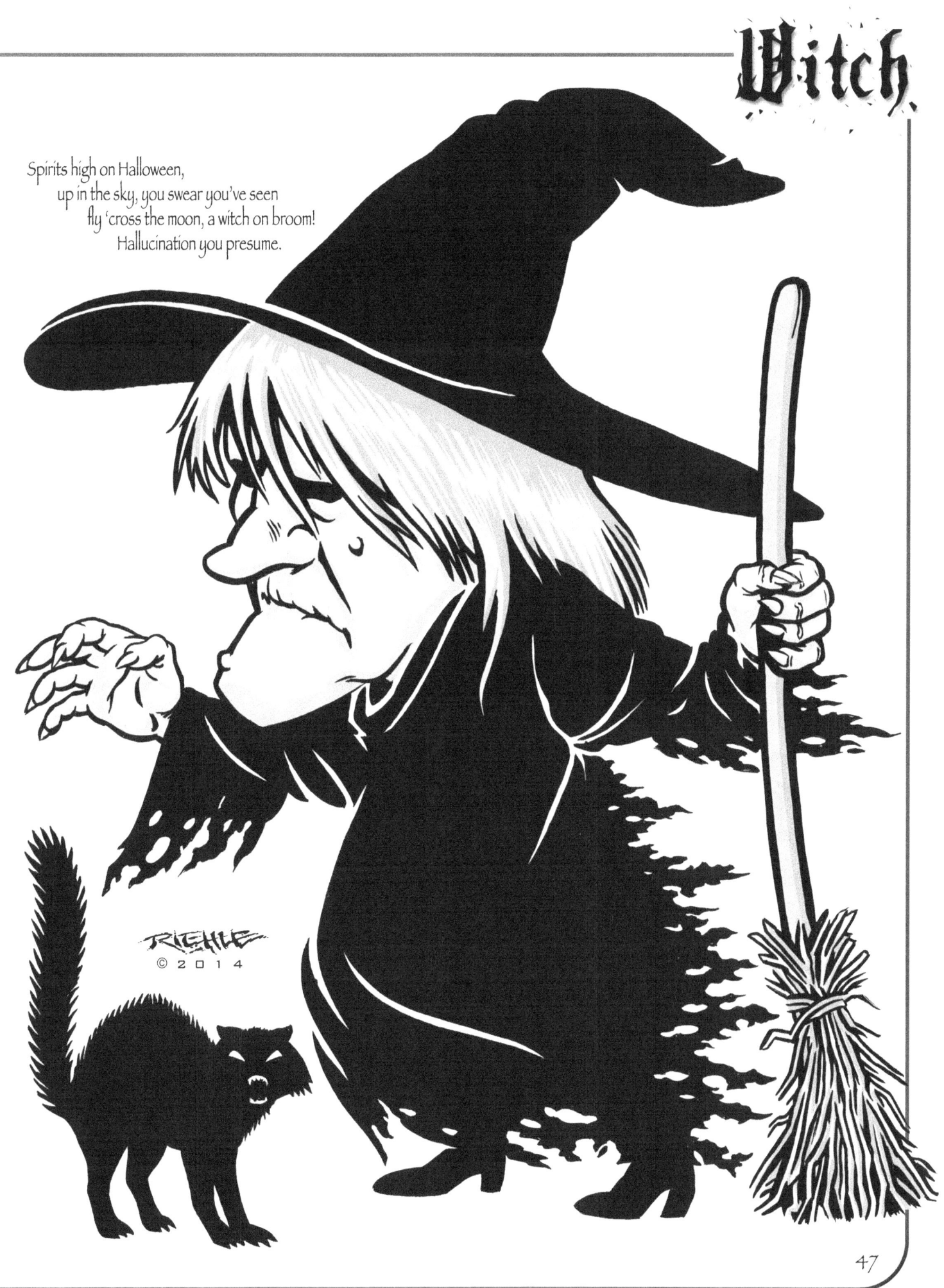

Swamp Monster

Down in the swamps and lowland bogs
it dwells with 'gators, snakes and frogs.
Rarely seen, few dare admit
to anyone that they've seen it.

RIEHLE
© 2014

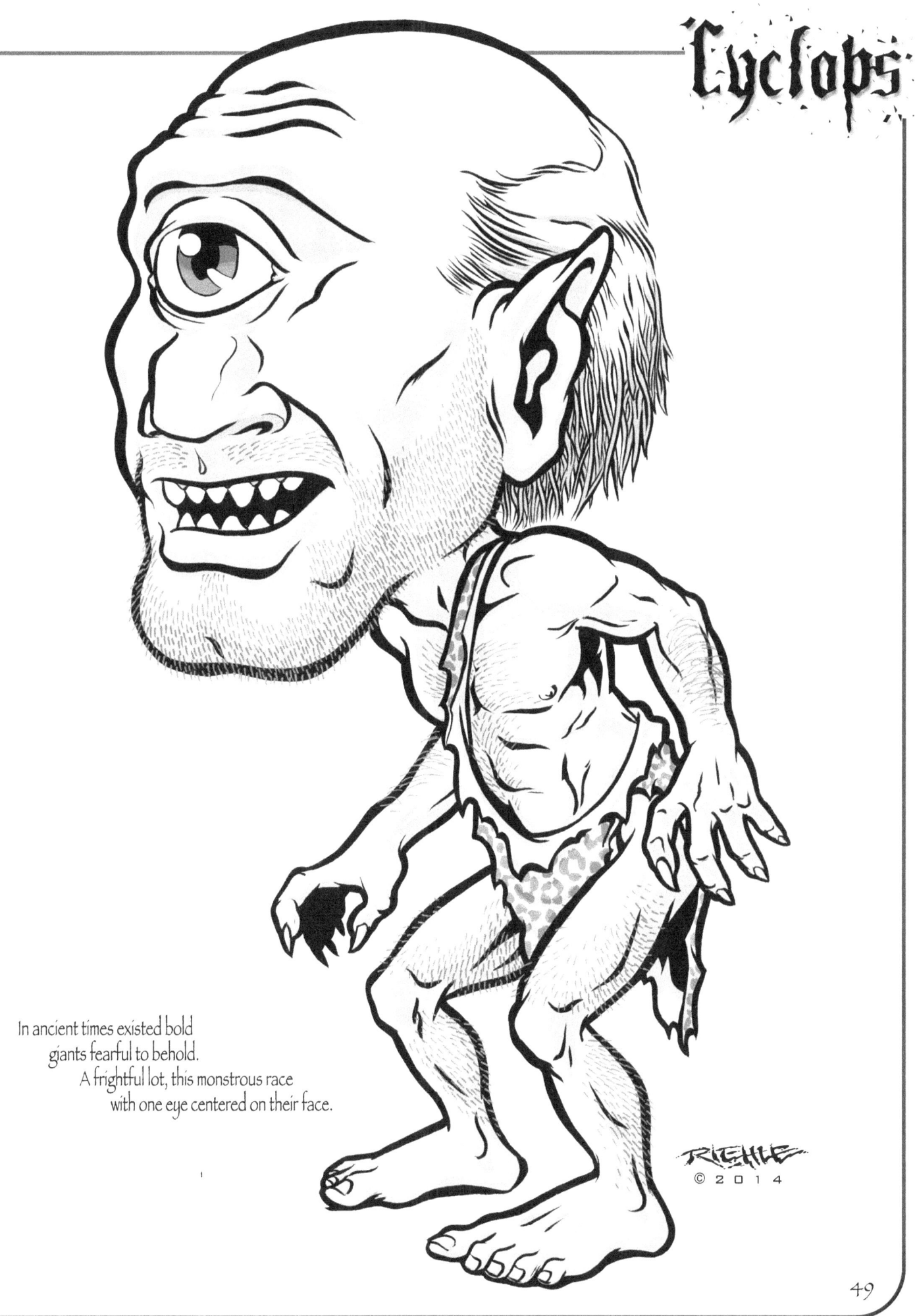

Cyclops

In ancient times existed bold
giants fearful to behold.
A frightful lot, this monstrous race
with one eye centered on their face.

RIEHLE
©2014

49

Demon

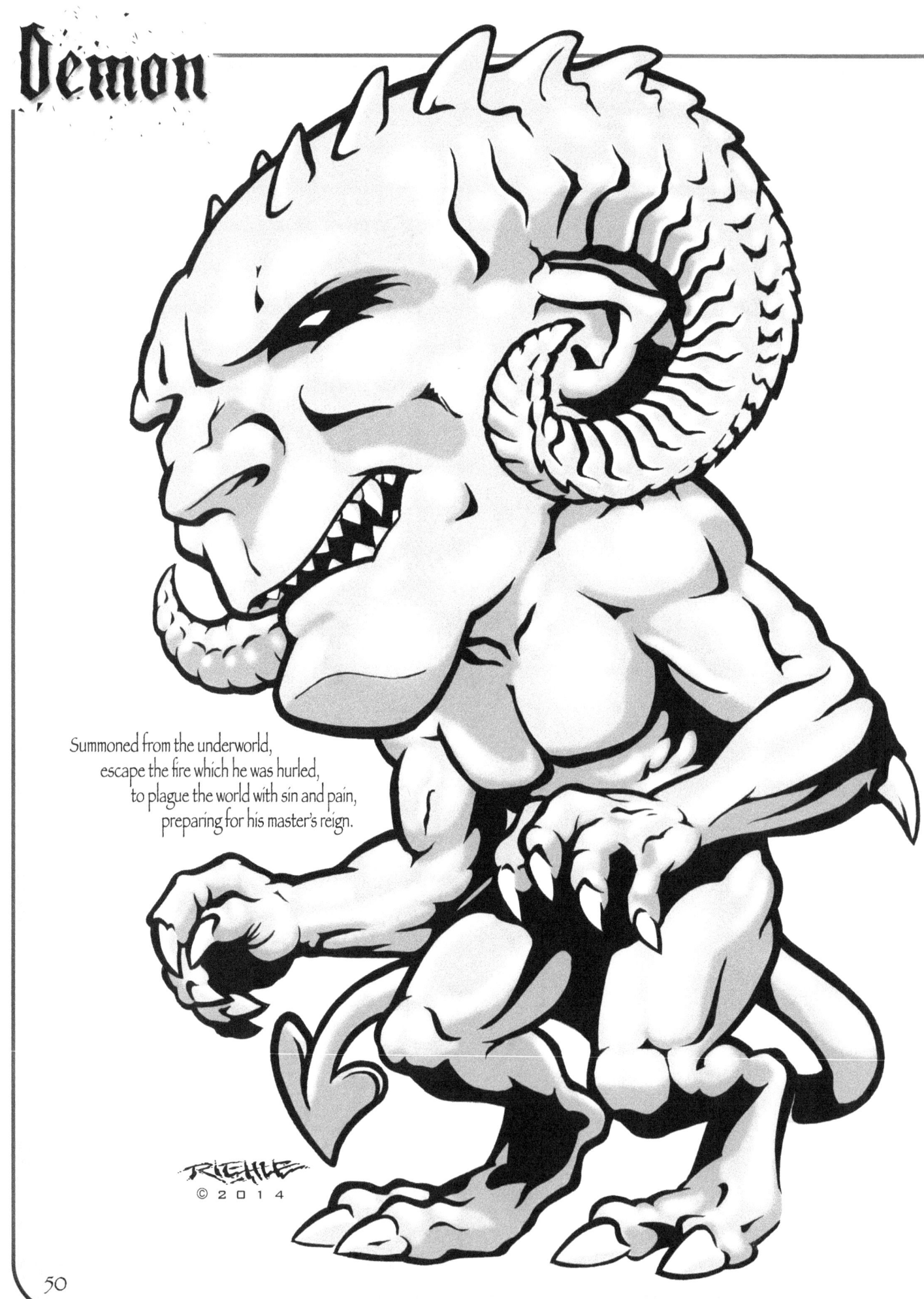

Summoned from the underworld,
escape the fire which he was hurled,
to plague the world with sin and pain,
preparing for his master's reign.

RICHIE
© 2014

Martian

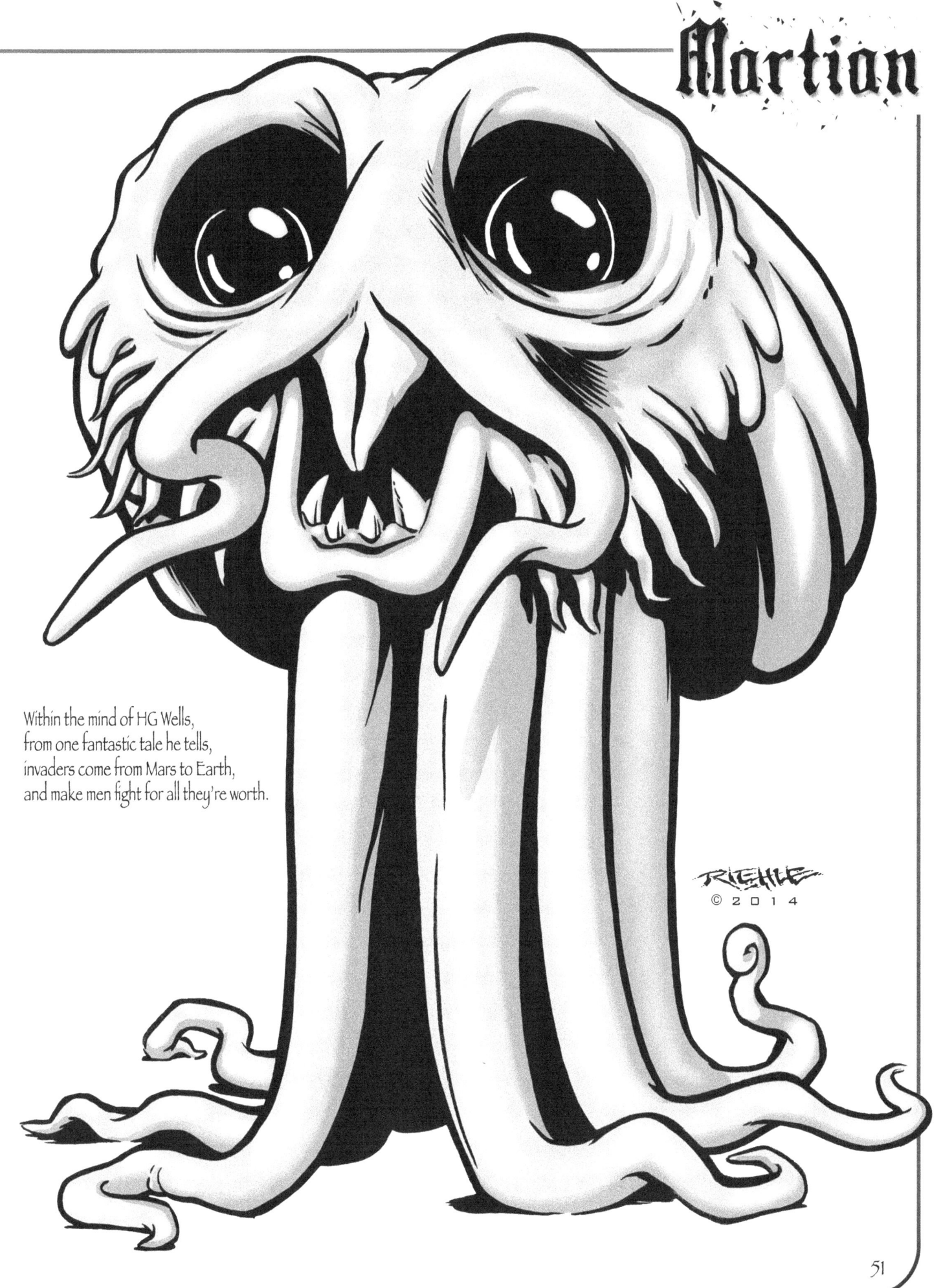

Within the mind of HG Wells,
from one fantastic tale he tells,
invaders come from Mars to Earth,
and make men fight for all they're worth.

RIEHLE
© 2 0 1 4

Daikaiju

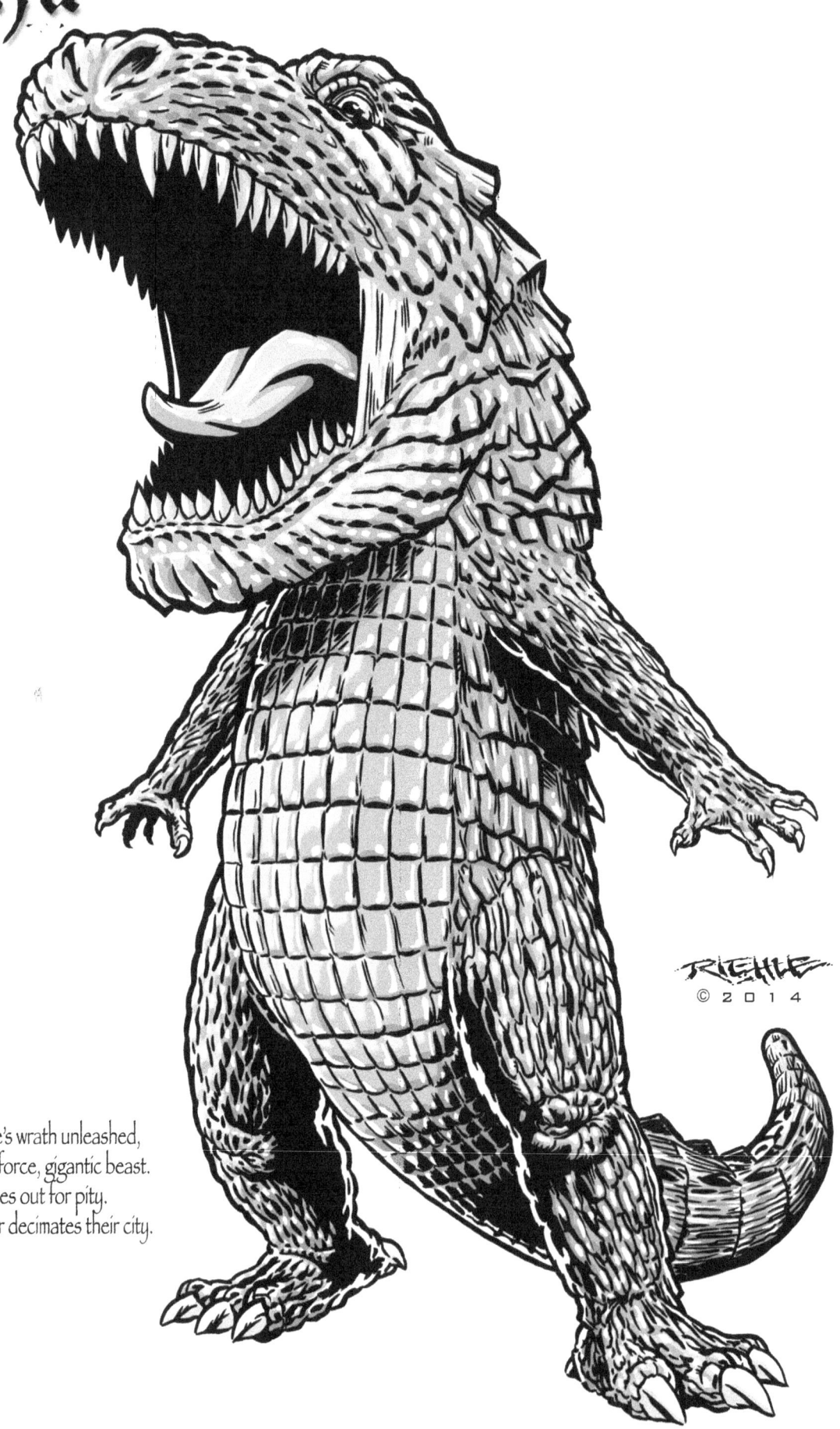

A force of nature's wrath unleashed,
destructive force, gigantic beast.
The populace cries out for pity.
The monster decimates their city.

RIEHLE
© 2 0 1 4

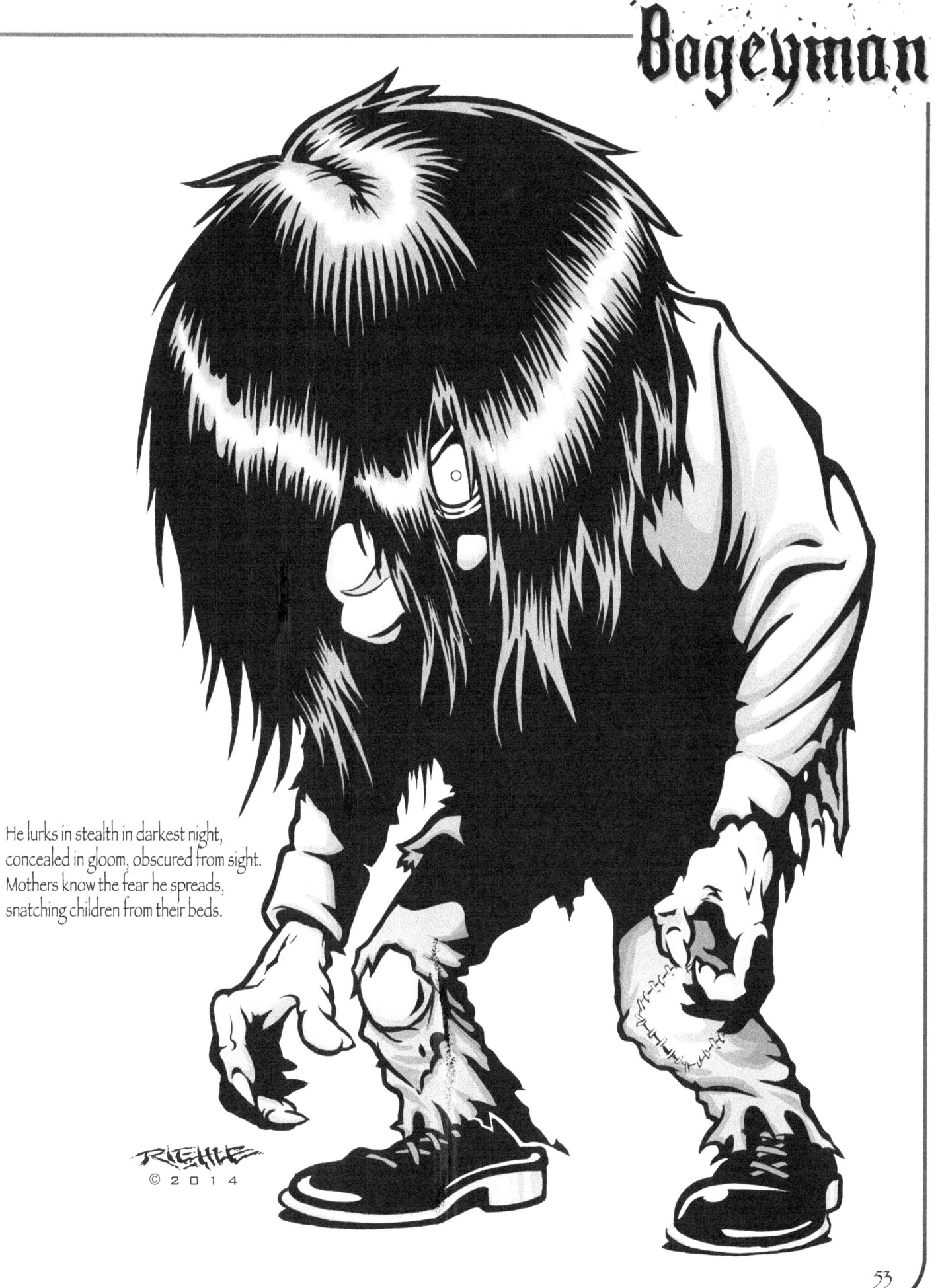

He lurks in stealth in darkest night,
concealed in gloom, obscured from sight.
Mothers know the fear he spreads,
snatching children from their beds.

Dracula

The prince of evil, legends say,
stalks the night and shuns the day.
Only blood will quell his thirst,
his victims will be reborn, cursed!

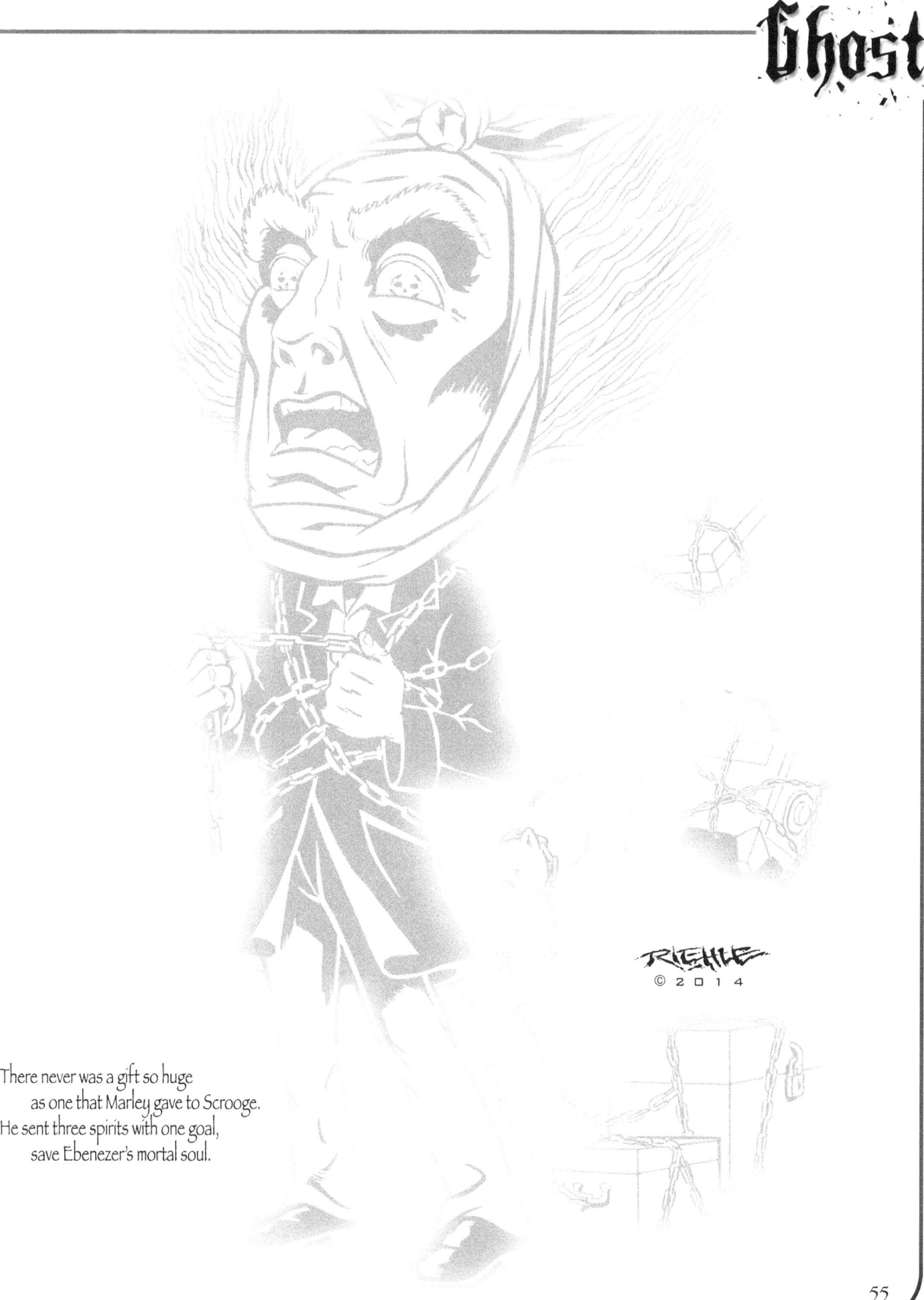

There never was a gift so huge
    as one that Marley gave to Scrooge.
He sent three spirits with one goal,
    save Ebenezer's mortal soul.

RIEHLE
© 2 0 1 4

LIST OF ILLUSTRATIONS

www.ingramcontent.com/pod-product-compliance
Lightning Source LLC
Chambersburg PA
CBHW080647180526
45168CB00008B/3338